THE COMPLEAT
LOW-COST
CAR RESTORATION
Vol. 1: Impressive Interiors
and
Vol. 2: Brilliant Bodies and Marvellous Mechanicals

Steve C. Brooks

Illustrations by Igor

Steve C. Brooks

Copyright © 2013 by Steven C. Brooks
Illustrations copyright © 2013 by Igor Spajic
This edition is Version 1.1
All rights reserved.

ISBN-13: 978-0-6487522-5-7

CONTENTS

VOL. 1: IMPRESSIVE INTERIORS

	INTRODUCTION	P. 1
1	PART 1. GET ORGANISED	P. 8
1.1	Overwhelm Overturned by Inventory	P. 8
1.2	Track Down a Tame Tradesman	P. 9
1.3	Protect Your Assets	P. 9
1.4	Brand Your Bags	P. 10
1.5	Paper Bags for Shiny Bits	P. 10
1.6	Plastic Bag Sandwich Protects Trims	P. 11
1.7	Join the Interior Parts Paparazzi	P. 11
2	PART 2. IMPROVING YOUR INSIDES	P. 13
2.1	Death-Rays and Car Interiors	P. 13
2.2	Your Plastics' False Friend	P. 14
2.3	Celica Interior Reborn	P. 14
2.4	The Philosophy of 'Heightened Reality' in Car Restoration	P. 15
2.5	Heightened Reality Examples	P. 17
2.6	Fixing the Dashboard	P. 19
2.7	Instrument Binnacle Repairs	P. 21
2.8	Makeover for Failing and Fading Switches	P. 24
2.9	Interior Repairs – VW Golf Hatchback Cover	P. 30
2.10	Brushed Aluminium or Stainless Steel Finish?	P. 32
2.11	New Contours for Old Seats	P. 33
2.12	Floor Foundations and Carpeting Capers	P. 34
2.13	General Interior Cleaning	P. 37
2.14	Deflector Screens Against Death Rays	P. 38

3	**PART 3. INTERIOR WARMTH THROUGH WONDERFUL WOODWORK**	P. 39
3.1	Creative Woodgraining	P. 39
3.2	Creating the Fake Timber Inlay	P. 45
3.3	Real Woodgraining – Restoring Real Wood	P. 48
3.4	Which Finish?	P. 49
3.5	Repairing Timber Veneer	P. 52
3.6	Stripping the Old Finish	P. 52
3.7	Types of Stain	P. 53
3.8	Applying a Lacquer Spray	P. 54
3.9	The First Seal Coat: The Lacquer Coat	P. 55
4	**PART 4. INVOLVING OTHERS AND A FINAL WRAP-UP**	P. 56
4.1	Spare Parts and Trim – Hunting and Gathering	P. 56
	VOL. 2: BRILLIANT BODIES AND MARVELLOUS MECHANICALS	P. 59
1	**PART 1. ORGANISE YOURSELF**	P. 59
1.1	One at a Time	P. 59
1.2	Your Garage Shopping List	P. 59
1.3	Bag It and Tag It	P. 61
1.4	Bubble Wrap Saves Surfaces from Accidental Damage	P. 63
1.5	Putting It Back Together	P. 63
1.6	Car Covers	P. 64
1.7	For Discarded Gucci Knock-Off Bags	P. 64

2	**PART 2. MECHANICALS & UNDERBODY**	P. 65
2.1	Degreasing Reveals the Awful Truth	P. 65
2.2	Rust-Proofing Brackets	P. 67
2.3	Masking Tape Stores Shavings	P. 68
2.4	Cuddling Your Coil	P. 68
2.5	Hoses Saved by Sacrificial Sheet	P. 69
2.6	Paint Lifts with Oven Cleaner	P. 73
2.7	Before You Paint the Engine	P. 73
2.8	Black Power Under the Hood	P. 75
2.9	A Clear Case for Gloss and Glamour	P. 76
2.10	Re-Energise Your Battery Tray	P. 77
2.11	Battery Negative – First and Last	P. 78
2.12	Going to Ground	P. 78
2.13	Repair Rusted Headlight Buckets	P. 78
2.14	Getting Under	P. 79
2.15	Undertaking the Undercoating	P. 80
2.16	Fix that Undercoating	P. 81
2.17	While You're There	P. 82

3	**PART 3. BODY WORKS**	P. 84
3.1	Doing Battle with the Rust Demon	P. 84
3.2	Removing Rust from Trunks or Boots	P. 87
3.3	When You've Found a Rust Hole	P. 88
3.4	Take a Bath	P. 92
3.5	Paintless Process for Panel Pounding	P. 93
3.6	Picnic Cutlery Protects Trim	P. 95
3.7	Happy Bolts Have Clean Threads	P. 95
3.8	Bright Idea for Bright Bolts	P. 96

3.9	Before You Spray	P. 96
3.10	Spraycan Painting	P. 97
3.11	Thin that Urethane	P. 97
3.12	Easy Pourer for Precious Paint	P. 98
3.13	Masking Materials for Spray Painting	P. 98
3.14	Tapes for Masking	P. 100
3.15	No Sway When You Spray	P. 101
3.16	Thinners for Covers	P. 101
3.17	Be a Grounded Person	P. 101
3.18	Keep a Count of Coats	P. 102
3.19	Perfection through Professional Paint Partnering	P. 102
3.20	Post-Painting Filing of Edges	P. 103
3.21	Wash Your Nylons	P. 103
3.22	Use the Card Guard	P. 104
3.23	Post-Painting Colour Sanding	P. 104
3.24	Post-Painting Polishing	P. 105
3.25	Polishing the Pre-Existing Paintwork	P. 106
3.26	Anti-Chipping Stripping	P. 107
3.27	Soap for Stripes	P. 109
3.28	Windscreen Scratches	P. 109
3.29	Window Seals' Secret Support	P. 110
3.30	Clean Your Plenum	P. 111
4	PART 4. APPEARANCE ITEMS	P. 113
4.1	Restoring Clear Plastic Badges and Emblems	P. 113
4.2	Restoring Clear Plastic Headlamp Lenses	P. 114
4.3	Repairing Chrome Trim	P. 114
4.4	Turn Signal and Brake Lamps in a New Light	P. 117

4.5	Restoring Chromed Badges	P. 118
4.6	Chroming – Pro and Con	P. 120
4.7	All That Glitters isn't Chrome	P. 121
5	**PART 5. WHEELS AND TYRES**	P. 122
5.1	The Menace of the Creeping Cover	P. 122
5.2	Wheeling and Cleaning	P. 125
5.3	Whitewall Tyres Scrub Up	P. 126
6	**PART 6. INVOLVING OTHERS AND A FINAL WRAP-UP**	P. 127
6.1	Spare Parts – Hunting and Gathering	P. 127
6.2	Domestic Car Restoration Etiquette	P. 128
6.3	Take Pity on Your Neighbours	P. 129
6.4	You've Finished – A Sense of Closure	P. 130
7	**PART 7. APPENDICES**	P. 133
7.1	APPENDIX A: TRADITIONAL MAINTENANCE	P. 133
7.2	APPENDIX B: EXTREME MAINTENANCE	P. 140
7.3	APPENDIX C: A WORD ON ALCOHOL IN FUEL	P. 154
7.4	Ethanol: Fuel or Fool?	P. 154

7.5	APPENDIX D: TIPS FOR HIGHER FUEL ECONOMY	P. 158
7.6	Only Idle Minds Idle	P. 159
7.7	Intelligent Braking	P. 159
7.8	Wiggling's No Drag	P. 160
7.9	Open Windows or Air Conditioning?	P. 160
7.10	Tune-Up with Water	P. 160
7.11	Moth Balls and Motors	P. 161
7.12	Two Coils Burn Oils	P. 162
7.13	Custom Ignition Timing for Factory Correct Performance	P. 163
7.14	Breathe Like an Athlete	P. 164
7.15	APPENDIX E: FURTHER RESOURCES FOR HIGH FUEL ECONOMY	P. 168
8	ABOUT THE AUTHOR	P. 169
9	CONTACT US	P. 169
10	DISCLAIMER	P. 169

INTRODUCTION

This isn't a guide on pimping your ride with bling and add-on gee-gaws. I am assuming that you wish to drive a car, not a Christmas tree. If your taste is all in your mouth, then you don't need a book like this. Return it for a refund!

This isn't a guide for the body shop or auto upholstery professional. There's a few out there already for the pro and aspiring pro. That's fine, but what about the rest of us?

The hot rodding and custom crowd who pursue perfection and have the bucks to do it won't find much of use here either. We also won't cover wild customising, since that is already covered in a variety of sources, and can be an expensive undertaking anyway. ("If it's metal, chrome it. If it's not being chromed, candy-apple it.")

We'll look into realistic methods and techniques that can be exploited at home with a modicum of skill and minimum of tools... and for low-buck outlays! This is becoming increasingly important as we enter an era of negative prosperity for many people. (I am paraphrasing that term beloved of economists – 'negative growth' – which is another way of saying 'recession'.)

We'll begin at the beginning.

There have been backyard mechanics since the dawn of the auto age, when it was the owners (or their staff) who were the main source of maintenance and refurbishing of motor cars. Often, owners were called upon to perform regular, complex maintenance and upkeep tasks.

Automobiles today don't require the same level of labour but there's also more complexity built into that set of wheels. And there's still wear and tear.

So what can the auto owner do to restore their car to better condition, if not quite to perfection? And what can be done in the home garage, with simple tools, and still keeping the car on the road for everyday use?

And for next to no money?

Sounds impossible? Unlikely? It's neither. There is a surprising amount of restoration that can be done on spare evenings or weekends, with small cash outlays, a modest collection of tools, some common household materials and a little bit of pluck.

And in this new era of underemployment, austerity and economic collapse, low-cost ways of doing things are more important than ever.

Interested?

Then join me and many others in a virtual underground community of low-cost, low-profile car restorers.

We'll begin with an important question.

Why?

Sure, this is a how-to guide. But it's also a why-to guide. And that may make this book unique outside the self-improvement literature. The best time to ask yourself 'why?' is at the beginning of a project.

Why are you restoring your car or truck? Is it to bring back memories of your childhood? Was it your Mom's or Dad's car? Does it remind you of a favourite uncle? Will the car be a gift to your son or daughter? To a friend or spouse or partner? Did you meet your first love in it? Is it the car you always wished you owned?

Is it to be able to present the finished restored car to a charity to raise raffle money for a worthy cause?

Are you restoring the car from an appreciation and love of beauty? Of art? Is it in the design and performance and character of the car?

Is it to keep the car going, functioning, fit for the purpose it was made for? This is seldom just transportation, so question any superficial answer you initially come up with.

Once you know why and what for, that will help you decide how much time and money you will be prepared to allocate to your restoration.

The Power of Intention

We ask the question 'why' before we get on with the business of 'how'. This is so important to begin with that I pose the question here.

Were you a kid riding in the back of a '66 Mercury wagon?

Do you remember a favourite uncle who would visit in his '66 Cadillac Calais hardtop sedan?

Is it art? You may think that the bat fins of the '59 Chevy Impala are tasteless, or you may applaud the flamboyance of an era long gone.

Are you perhaps reclaiming your youth with a '71 Buick GS Sport Coupe?

Once you've answered these questions to your satisfaction, go and get some quotes for any specialised work you need like chrome plating or spray painting or an automatic transmission rebuild. Ask the tradesmen what they need from you in order to get the best results. For example, in this book we cover surface preparation before a panel is painted. Discover what you can do to reduce the paid-for time of these professionals. Also ask to talk to their prior customers. A quality establishment is proud of its work and won't hesitate to give you some references.

What is your budget? If it blew out by 50% (which it could easily do) are you still able to complete your restoration goals? Will it simply take longer than anticipated?

Do you have a reasonable working space? Is it clean? You won't be there 24/7 so can you protect your project from the weather when you're working or sleeping?

Set your restoration goals only according to their importance to you, not to someone else. Write them down as a series of small steps.

Or are you just freshening up a cute, daily runabout, like this 2002 VW New Beetle?

Once you know and have a clear idea on what you want to achieve, who it's for and why, that will guide your decisions further down the track, such as how much money to spend or time to lavish on the project, or which people to involve.

Into classic cars? A cool Thunderbird from 1966 is a classy choice.

Are you into quirky cars? 1976 produced this AMC Gremlin, which relied on simple mechanicals in a compact package. Afros are optional.

PART 1. GET ORGANISED

Overwhelm Overturned by Inventory

Now there's a hurdle most of us face when dealing with a car restoration (or other major project). Rational planning for the project goes out the window when emotion takes over.

It's easy to feel overwhelmed with a massive restoration project.

Where do you begin? What do you spend?

Be clear about the fixes you want to see to by writing them on a list. Split the tasks into smaller ones. For example, 'fix interior' would break down into 'fix speedometer bezel', 'sand driver's side wooden door trim', 'varnish driver's side wooden door trim', 'renew parcel shelf carpet' and so on.

Once you have any necessary tools and materials for a task, do that task – start to finish. COMPLETE THE FIRST TASK BEFORE STARTING THE SECOND.

There's nothing worse than treading on a conveyor belt of jobs with no let up and no end in sight. (Sounds too much like work, huh?) Finish your task then take a break. Give yourself a little reward. (A LITTLE reward!) Celebrate your progress in minor increments. Acknowledge to yourself that you've finished it by ticking it off your list.

Most repairs, modifications or upgrades are unseen. A repair is successful when it doesn't look like there's a repair. So refer back to your list. It doesn't even matter much if you add more restoration and repair tasks to your list, provided you see those ticks against completed tasks. They'll remind you of what you've achieved and how far you've come, no matter what stage of the project you're in.

Track Down a Tame Tradesman

This book focuses on low-cost things you can do to restore, improve and upgrade your vehicle's interior. The next book in this series will cover mechanicals and body work.

With this focus in mind, auto upholsterers are the paid professionals here and in some cases, you will need their professional help. But there is a lot you can do first to prepare the foundations, so to speak, before you need to call them in. That way, your labour bill will be reduced substantially.

When choosing an upholsterer, ask to see their prior work. Do they specialise in an area of upholstery you need? Can they give you any satisfied customers to talk to? Will they work with you by advising you on what preparations you can make that will make their job quicker, easier (and cost less)?

Good tradesmen and women are already sought after, with their schedule books full of clients. They don't need additional business from you, so should be happy to explain what they need from you in order to finish your project with a minimum of fuss and outlay.

Protect Your Assets

I mean your personal assets here. And no, I don't mean THAT personal.

I mean your eyes, for example. Some tasks relating to interior restorations may involve flicks of solvents or sprays or falling grit. Protect your eyes with a pair of goggles. There are varieties of different plastic goggles that can be bought from hardware stores. Most of the time you won't need them but there will be just that once that you'll wish you were wearing them. Save yourself the aggravation.

Save your back too. If seats are being removed or returned to your interior, ask for help. They may not be heavy (or may as the case may be) but sure are awkward to manoeuvre. An extra pair of hands will make the job easier and probably save you from damaging something or scraping paint off a door jamb.

A lot of automobile interior work occurs at the vehicle's floor level, or just above it. Instead of bending down or kneeling AND bending down, use a low stool to sit on. A small cushion can also be used and it will prevent your ass from going numb. It can be an outdoor furniture cushion, which should have an easily cleanable surface. Rest the cushion on a clean tarpaulin or wrap it in a plastic shopping bag to protect it from dirt.

Brand Your Bags

When taking apart interior assemblies, you will be removing clusters of screws, bolts and minor attachment pieces. These can be easily lost, misplaced or mistaken for other fasteners. As you remove them, place them in small bags and label the bags. Anything from a kitchen freezer bag to a zip-lock sandwich bag will do. Plastics are best because you can see through them and you can write directly on them with a felt marker.

You can set aside the bags in a box or drawer for interior parts. Or you can use masking tape and actually attach the bags to the interior trim panel or large assembly they belong to. That way, you always know where to look when the time comes to re-assemble these parts.

You can't be too anally retentive about this – methodical filing and storing is the key to fast, hassle-free re-assembly.

Paper Bags for Shiny Bits

For those chrome-plated or steel fasteners or bolts, or inside mirrors, sometimes it's better to store them in paper bags than plastic. Particularly if you live in a humid environment. Plastic acts as a moisture barrier but what moisture gets in can't escape easily and rust or corrosion is the result.

The best preserved mechanical parts were those that used to be lightly oiled then enclosed in paper wrappings. They can be put on a shelf for decades and when unwrapped still look new.

You can 'oil' your shiny parts with WD40 and put them in a paper bag.

And hope that it won't take you decades before you need them.

Plastic Bag Sandwich Protects Trims

In your interior restoration project, you may need to remove door trim panels and other linings and stand them against a wall in your garage. They may have delicate bright metal trims which might catch and bend on an obstruction or cloths which could tear from contact with a sharp edge.

You can protect your interior panels with layers of plastic bags from supermarkets. Tape them lightly to the panels they protect. Bunch them up if you need a cushioning effect.

Join the Interior Parts Paparazzi

In an increasingly shallow popular culture, what celebrities get up to is slavishly followed by many people. And the paparazzi are there to provide them with pictures. Was there a face lift? Is that a baby bump? Has weight been gained? Lost? All these burning questions might be answered with before and after shots, sometimes taken with telephoto lenses.

What you can do during your restoration is to become a paparazzo to your interior. You can record what it looks like before you take it apart for its 'makeover'. (And you won't need telephoto lenses!)

Today more than ever, electronic media are part of our lives, so use them in your car's interior restoration. Reading this e-book on a Kindle is a good start of course, but take a smart phone or digital camera and snap photos of details before you take things apart. Macro lenses are most useful here.

Most workshop manuals may not cover all aspects of car interiors and their disassembly. They focus on mechanical and body engineering and leave out the soft stuff. Take close-up photos of the way rubber seals are attached to the doors or window openings. Take a photo of how the carpet folds into a corner. Record how the wiring rests under the dashboard. How a seatbelt retractor box is bolted in.

Download the pictures to your computer and label them too. That way, they're on more than one device and are less likely to get wiped accidentally. File them in appropriate folders so you can come back and find them easily.

You get the picture: take lots of pictures!

Join the ranks of the Interior Parts Paparazzi. It saves you head-scratching detective work later on.

PART 2. IMPROVING YOUR INSIDES

Death-Rays and Car Interiors

Disintegrator rays date back in science fiction to 1928 with the publication of the first Buck Rogers novel (he entered comic strips the next year). These death-ray weapons would blast all material objects into their component atoms.

Your automobile's not likely to encounter a disintegrator gun attack, but the same damage a hostile spaceman could do in a second is done in slow motion over a period of years. And it's done by the sun.

The ultraviolet rays do the most damage, attacking the plasticisers in vinyl, plastic and synthetic rubber. Plasticisers are those components of plastics that keep them plastic, that is, flexible. The radiation breaks down longer chain molecules first, then the shorter ones. Once molecular bonds are broken, the substance falls apart. In effect, it becomes brittle, cracks and splits into tinier and tinier pieces.

Ultra-violet can't get through glass, so although your external rubber seals, plastic bumpers and tyres are out in the open, that protects your upholstery somewhat.

However, infra-red rays heat up everything, inside or out. Making substances hotter releases the volatile elements in plastics that keep them soft and supple – those plasticisers again.

Some substances have sacrificial elements to take the brunt of the sun's attack. The first car tyres were cream coloured because that was the colour of the natural latex they were made from. These tyres were prone to sunburn, like we are, but unlike our skin pigmentation, once these natural rubber tyres were sunburnt, they couldn't recover. They became brittle, at first on the outside. A brittle tyre doesn't last very long in normal use. Later, carbon black was added as a sacrificial element, both to add some structural strength and to protect the natural rubber from the UV rays. When your tyres go brownish, that's the result of losing some carbon black to UV radiation exposure.

Pigments in (synthetic) rubber seals and in vinyl can protect the underlying substance, but only to a point. Once it's gone, it has to be replaced. That's easier said than done.

Your Plastics' False Friend

You can't use a popular protectant with a brand name that begins with an 'A' or anything else based on silicon oils. These oils replace the plasticisers, but are worse than useless. The silicon oils are even more volatile and short-lived than the plasticisers. So you have to keep re-applying them at short intervals and keep buying the product. A good idea for repeat business but not a good idea for the health of your vinyl and plastics.

I use '303 Protectant', which is specifically designed to replace plasticisers – with plasticisers. It's not available everywhere, but I use nothing else.

Legal disclaimer: I have no business relationship with the makers of '303 Protectant'. As I've used it, so I recommend it as a much better alternative to the run-of-the-mill silicon oil stuff. And they haven't paid me anything to recommend it to you. The bastards!

Celica Interior Reborn

When I began restoring my wife's Celica RA40 Liftback, I was starting with an awful interior. Interior plastic panels were disintegrating into powder – literally – and a lot of the original colour impregnated into the material had been bleached out as well.

After many trips to the wrecker's where a number of Celicas were then available, I chose the best interior parts and panels I could find. Some were in blue (my car's interior colour) and some in black or tan.

I would need to paint them to match my interior, but this would require a panel beater mixing some special, colour-matched paint. I also needed to re-paint my faded blue panels. Since I was doing a very low-buck restoration, I decided to find the closest available blue out of a spray can. I found a medium-blue, gloss, spray enamel and bought several cans.

I sprayed one thin coat first, then another. The colour on the surface became brighter, and by varying the thickness and number of coats, I was able to colour-match the finish on several panels, all from different coloured interiors. The blue I had chosen was a gloss enamel colour, so it would cover the surface and fill in any imperfections.

The interior plastics all had a leather-grain surface texture, so it was important not to fill the texture in with too much enamel 'body'. My technique was very forgiving. If I found myself with a spray coat too thick and heavy in spots, the 'pooling' of the paint was quickly repaired. While still wet, I dabbed the excess off with a clean, lint-free rag, or I used that most flexible of tools, the human fingertip. Just a series of light touches was enough to remove the excess. Then a light spray almost immediately over the area, while the underlying paint was still wet, was enough to hide the error. All the wet paint flowed together, then dried together and became uniform.

I had now achieved two things:

(a.) I had introduced a new coating that would protect the plastic panels from further UV-caused surface disintegration; and

(b.) I had colour-matched and freshened the interior.

And I had done this for next to no cost.

Mind you, the blue was brighter in hue than the factory's more subdued, darker shade. But it was close, and it made the interior less shaded. I call it 'Heightening Reality'.

The Philosophy of 'Heightened Reality' in Car Restoration

What's heightening reality? It's when Tony Curtis plays Harry Houdini in a biographical movie. Or Tom Cruise playing Colonel Claus von Stauffenberg (Hitler's would-be assassin) in the film *Valkyrie*; or

Leonardo DiCaprio as Howard Hughes in '*Aviator*', again both bio-pics. In other words, a real person played by an actor who is more handsome or beautiful than the original.

Hey, virtually every Hollywood movie (and EVERY Bollywood movie) is 'Heightened Reality'. You wouldn't watch it if it looked like your own life, now would you?

Heightened Reality is giving you more of what you already have. A matt finish can become satin; a satin finish gloss. (But a matt finish should not jump to a gloss.) Unpainted alloys can be polished then sealed with a clear, gloss urethane finish. They won't oxidise, are easier to clean, and look more attractive.

With such detailing, use this rule of thumb: If the factory wanted to do it, but chickened out because it would cost a couple of cents extra per part, you can do it yourself.

But it's sometimes a fine line. A car underside finished all in gloss black is not Heightened Reality. It's just a bit *gauche*. So is chroming every mechanical part. What belongs on a hot rod built for show not go, does not belong on your car. (Remember the Kool Kustomiser's Kreed? "If it's Metal, Chrome It. If It's Not Being Chromed, Candy-Apple It.")

The context can also change what's reality and what's Heightened Reality. I'll explain that with a story.

A few years ago, my wife and I toured New Zealand and stopped by a small car museum in the North Island. The curator told us the story of a black Ford Model T on display there. I had noticed the paint runs on the rear of the Tudor sedan body. The curator explained that the car had been restored by an old man who knew Model Ts as a boy. He had it taken to a local panel beater's for the spray painting. When the car was finished, the old owner inspected the work. He asked the painter to do the work again.

There hadn't been anything wrong with the paint finish. But that was the point – it was *too* good. The owner had received Heightened Reality when he actually didn't want it.

You see, the Model Ts that the owner remembered were all mass produced at a cracking pace. The men in the paint shop had to cover the bodies with their spray guns and move on to the next unit on the assembly line. There were always some imperfections in the paint finish, and this included runs of overspray.

So the old bloke got his authentic, imperfect Model T in the end, complete with runs in the paint finish. That's dedication – not to Heightened Reality but to Hyper-Reality. And that's a discourse for another time.

Heightened Reality Examples

I have explained the philosophy of 'Heightened Reality' and how it guides your car restoration or improvement. I wrote that Heightened Reality is giving you more of what you already have. Also that if the factory wanted to do it, but chickened out because it would cost a couple of cents extra per part, you can do it yourself.

Here are a couple of specific examples that may serve as more guidance.

My wife's RA40 Celica Liftback came with factory air-conditioning, which was overhauled and worked well. In our foraging expeditions to the wreckers', I had seen that the RA40 Coupes were a lower-spec model than the Liftbacks. They had plastic instead of vinyl side arm-rest panels in the rear; radio instead of radio-tape deck; and no air-conditioning. *Quel horreur!*

But the Coupes had an extra parcel shelf under the dashboard on the passenger side, which the Liftback didn't have on account of its air-conditioning assembly. They also had a little parcel tray that went where the Liftback's (separate) tape deck would have gone. I bought both from the wreckers. Why?

I had already installed a combined radio-tape deck where the factory radio went in the dashboard. This freed the space for the storage cubbyhole that would have been taken up by a useless (not working) original tape deck. Bonus storage!

I found that the extra parcel shelf had score marks on the underside, which when cut would have removed part of the back of the tray. This enabled it to fit around the air-conditioner assembly. The factory could have supplied it, but chose not to, just to save a few cents per car. Still more bonus storage!

What compromises did the factory build into your car which you don't have to put up with? Some markets got all the goodies, other markets made do with fewer features.

Another case in point.

My first car was a 1976 VW Golf 3-door hatchback. A Teutonically efficient design, but locally assembled (Australia), it was a veritable *schitbox* of thin carpet, cardboard hatchback luggage cover and non-opening rear side windows. The efficient VW flow-through ventilation simply couldn't operate with closed windows. This in a hot country like Australia!

So, I had some room for improvements.

I like the convenience of intermittent wipers. The Golf didn't come with intermittent wiper control. Sell it and buy another car with this feature? Not necessary.

I had a very detailed workshop manual which covered international variations of Golfs and Sirocco coupes. The fuse and relay panel had a space for an intermittent wiper relay. I took the manual to an auto electrician and we examined the three-pronged plug holes set aside for it.

BEFORE

AFTER

He looked at the wiring diagram. He found an intermittent wiper relay can for a Japanese car which would fit. We plugged it in to see if it would work. It did!

So I drove away with the only 1976-77 Golf in Australia with intermittent wipers. I don't know when following generations of locally available Golfs got around to having this feature. And it only cost me about $18 (multiply that by three for today's inflated dollar value). You can bet that I talked up this feature when I sold the car, as well I might. And I believe that it added to the resale value.

Did your model come with an upmarket variation

with leather upholstery? Would you like to replace your cloth interior with a leather version? Ring around and go to the wrecker that has it. Unbolt it all yourself, taking care to make sure that all under-seat track springs are fully extended. Otherwise, one track assembly may thrust its bayonet of a sharp-edged seat track at you! And when you least expect it. I know – it happened to me and I was lucky to escape with only a painful cut in the palm of my hand.

Choose the appropriate colour for your interior/exterior if there's a choice. If not, some neutral colour like grey or black. You can re-colour leathers and vinyls later, but it's an extra step and a hassle and cost you should try and avoid. Recolouring upholstery must be done well otherwise it looks like crap. Vinyl is easier to re-colour, but leather should be left to an experienced person.

Why stop at the front seats? Get the rear leather seats, and the upmarket door panels as well. In fact, the front kick panels and everything. A colour-coded ceiling? Grab that too.

Keep all the screws used to mount interior parts and panels. If you can, use masking tape to keep the screws in place once the part or panel has been removed. There's no doubt then as to which screw or fastener goes where. For the other screws, as you remove them, keep them in a small plastic bag or a re-sealable sandwich bag. (Without a sandwich in it.)

Are there adjustment motors and controls in the front seats? Are there covered-up plugs in your car already there to take the upscale power seats? Does your car's fuse box accommodate the extra power seat circuits? Will simply plugging in these power seats give you these extra comforts? Find out before going to the wrecker's!

Complete the transformation: take the little badges on the inside and outside that denote the upmarket version of your car, and fix them to yours in the same places.

So take a moment to think about how you can incrementally improve your ride to a place of Heightened Reality. What holes are there yet to be (ahem) plugged?

Fixing the Dashboard

Plastic dashboards have a tendency to crack. It's all that heat and occasional UV light that attacks the surface – and underneath. (See above for how this happens and for some methods of coping with this.)

Some dashboards have cracks with the aspect of canyons. Beneath the surface layer is normally a plastic sponge-like body. This sort of compound is designed for collision protection, so that occupants of the car if unbelted are flung onto surfaces which will 'give', deforming and absorbing impact forces.

Now, we can improve the dashboard surface at least, with a sheet of vinyl. You can buy a sheet off the roll at the local fabric shop. Measure out the width of your dashboard and the depth. Buy a bit more than you think you'll need (enough for two attempts?) Saves you a second trip to the store. Usually, black vinyl fabric will suffice for all instances.

Sometimes, you can colour match your car interior with a choice from a limited range of vinyl colours. To add an extra layer of effort, the vinyl itself can be coloured with special flexible vinyl paints. These are available in spray cans, in an admittedly limited range of colours (black, red, white, blue…a green?) A better option might be colour-matching using custom mixed paints. A paint specialist, or auto body shop paint supplier, might be able to help here. Paint it before installation of course.

Now that you have your vinyl cloth, ask your partner very nicely for her sewing expertise. Basically, it is a question of tailoring. The sheet must be made to conform to the various curves and planes of the dashboard piece. Sometimes the dashboard overlay (the softer part) is easily removable with a few screws. Other times it's hard. It may be possible to recover it without removing it. It's a case by case basis.

You will need a good adhesive and some judicious stitching. A sewing machine helps here. When the vinyl reaches an edge, fold over and secure it.

Air vents can be ignored for now. Once the sheet is in place if only temporarily, mark the air vent slots out on the sheet in soft crayon. Trace their outlines carefully. When the time comes to open up the vents, cut along the incision marks you have previously made. One straight incision along the length of the vent will usually do, but you may need to cut diagonally into the corners. Now take the resulting flaps and shape them around the inner surfaces of the vents. Use contact glue to keep these flaps in place and to prevent them from peeling off later. You don't want to cover these air vents with poorly placed edges or curling up vinyl sheet.

Sometimes the outlet grilles are easily removable for the fitting and when replaced will help keep your new vinyl overlay in place.

Try a thin layer of sponge rubber (a thin layer!) and cut it out in sections, and do a dry run by placing it here and there on the dashboard surfaces. Try covering it with the vinyl cloth, securing temporarily with masking tape. Look at the result. Is it softer and padded looking? Is it excessively padded and looking stuffed? (Is this the pimped-up look you secretly want anyway?)

When you're satisfied with the result, then go for it. First use a spray adhesive for the sheet sponge rubber, and put it firmly in place. Once it's there, you're ready for the vinyl covering installation.

Finally, inspect your work (and your partner's). Does the vinyl look factory? Is it straight and has the sponge rubber been doubled over by mistake? Before you glue it down for sure, see to the edges and corners.

Use clamps to hold it down where you can, or masking tape or duct tape where you cannot. Any adhesive from this tape can be cleaned off later. The point is to keep all the vinyl edges down while the glue sets.

Once it's all done, thank your partner and her sewing machine and skills. Buy her some flowers or cook dinner for her.

Instrument Binnacle Repairs

We've fixed the top of the dashboard with a fitted sheet of vinyl, possibly with a layer of plastic foam underneath. Now let's turn our attention to the gauges and instrument binnacle.

There may be cracks, scratches or chipped edges around the instruments or elsewhere on the dashboard.

If the plastic is black or has its colour impregnated in the substance, you can use a mild polish to take the scratches out.

Cracks can be filled in with putty, then when it's dry, carefully sanded down to a smooth surface. You can use a nail file for a variety of these repairs. The metal files (only use the disposable emery file if you have to) have different grades of abrasiveness on each side, so you can choose which you start and finish off with.

A fine grit wet-and-dry sandpaper of 88 grit up to about 1200 grit is ideal for these tiny repairs. You can smooth down the surface until it's equal to any shiny plastic.

Once you're satisfied with your putty repair, and it's dry, an undercoat can be applied with a fine brush. This time, do use a good artist's brush, made from sable or suchlike fine, natural hair. Hey, you're doing fine artistic work here aren't you? Use a #1 or #0 or even a #00 or #000 size brush, as you're doing delicate work, not covering acres of surface.

First lay down a drop sheet or cloth underneath where you will be touching up in your car interior. This will usually be the carpet or some other flat surface. Use junk mail shiny paper, but newspaper is acceptable, as you're not spray-painting, and those loose fibres will not get in the way of the small brush repairs you'll be doing.

If the undercoat is in a spray can, you can still use the little brush to apply it. Have some mineral turpentine handy if it's an enamel, or thinners if it's a lacquer, and a clean rag. Of course, water, if it's an acrylic.

Shake the can well for at least 30 seconds, changing hands. Use this as a form of exercise. Spray the can into the inside of the cap it came with. Hold the cap at an angle so that the small amount of paint has pooled in the bottom. Dip your brush in this little pool and paint your repair.

Many spraycan caps have a breather hole in the perimeter. Of course, avoid pooling the paint here otherwise it may drip through onto a seat surface or other expletive-coaxing area.

If you have a number of repair spots to paint over, spray some more into the spraycan cap and continue. Remember to clean the brush with your solvent and rag from time to time as the paint may harden among the bristles, making your brush less flexible and less able to pick up fresh paint. With lacquer, clean the brush every minute or so.

Wait for the undercoat to dry before applying paint. Don't rush these things. You can still drive the car if it's on the road, or do other restoration work if it's off. The solvent in an enamel paint will attack the putty and granulate the surface if the putty's still not completely dry.

Of course, if you're repairing a control knob or switch surface, you will have to take into account the likely length of your repair and when you next want to use the vehicle.

Use the same brush (clean of course) and apply the paint colour over your repaired spots. Feather the paint over the edges of the puttied repair, but be mindful of the 'body' of the paint. An enamel is relatively thick compared with a lacquer.

If they're small enough, chipped edges can be repaired to their former straight sharpness with fine putty. Apply some with the pointy tip of the nail file. Use it like a miniature trowel. When the putty's dry, use the nail file to smooth the surfaces and have them meet at a sharp edge.

What putty am I referring to? I have used model kit putty for these small jobs. Why not? The scale of the work is about the same size as for scale models. A model airplane seam between the wing and fuselage would be about the same size as the auto repairs I'm describing.

Raid your son's model kit paints and supplies for an undercoat, brushes, and possibly colour as well. Or buy them from a hobby shop. There are a number of different available colours, so you may be able to colour-match to your requirements. The tins of paint are quite small but they will be adequate for your needs.

You can custom-colour-match if you choose by mixing from two of these tins of paint on a smooth or glossy surface, using it as an artist's palette, until you have the right hue or shade. Use toothpicks to pick up drops of paint from each tin. Use a different toothpick for each, you don't want to go mixing the paints accidentally in their own tins.

Mix on the palette with a third toothpick. Make an appropriate amount of correct colour to cover the spots you have in mind, at least twice over. If the colour has to battle to match the surroundings, more than one coat will be needed.

You can re-coat within a short time, depending on the paint you're using, or after something like three hours, or even days later. Usually, recoating instructions are printed on the little tins themselves. Ask the staff at your hobby shop if you've bought them there. Or ask your son!

Use the tip of your nail file to lever open the lids of the tins and use sturdy toothpicks to mix the paint within. Ensure they are well mixed before dipping your brush.

Try to match the surroundings. If it's a glossy plastic, make it glossy. If it's satin or matt, match that. You can buy many hobby paint colours in different finishes.

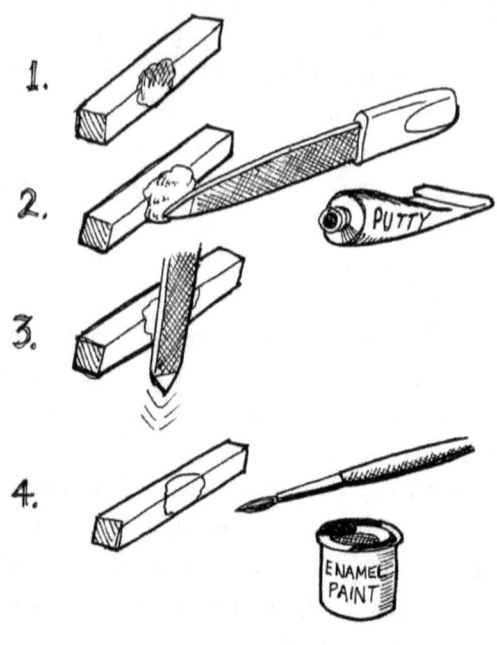

Once done, the repairs should be indistinguishable from their surrounding surfaces. Use a fingertip's size of very smooth sandpaper (about 1000 grit) to smooth down any excess around the repair, keeping away from the painted repair.

Curved surfaces with sharp edges can also be repaired using these same techniques. All you need is time, patience and a very small amount of materials, for a repair you can be proud of.

If you're a perfectionist, you'll still know where the repair is. But no one else will!

Makeover for Failing and Fading Switches

Let's zoom in further here. You've fixed the dashboard and instrument binnacle. If any gauge isn't working, that requires specialised knowledge which we won't go into here. However, if switches aren't cooperating with their job description, there's a surprising amount that can be done by the amateur.

Switches are like traffic lights – they direct electrical current either one way or the other. At some point, they stop the current too. Switches need to be able to carry that current and also to be operated by simple and positive movements.

An extra requirement for switches made in thousands or tens of thousands of copies - such as for auto manufacturers - is that they must be cheap and quick to manufacture.

I was faced with the problem of replacing window lift switches in my Rover. I would get a window to lower, but not to raise. This was very inconvenient, as you may imagine. These were rocker type switches, operating only when pressed by a fingertip.

I rang around and found that replacements were either second-hand or expensive originals. Some were simply not available. I was determined to get around this all too typical situation.

You may be able to find matching switches at a wrecker's yard. If so, jackpot! Remove them all and store them in your garage, properly labelled. They don't take up much storage space and can save a lot of time and hassle later.

If the switches in your auto are hard to find from a supplier or a wrecker's yard, see if you can swap them around. Sometimes the internals and body of a switch are the same as other switches in your car, with the only difference being the markings on the button. If they operate in the same way, plug into the same contacts and look alike, then a simple swap is all you need. Swap a less-used switch for a commonly-used one. You can then attend to the faulty switch in the less-used position sometime later.

Sometimes the switches work the same way but have different contact pins underneath. I found this out with my Rover: back door switches look the same as the front door switches but wouldn't swap with the front because the pins underneath differed. But at least the switch buttons could be detached and swapped between switches as needed. I was getting somewhere.

To my suggestion of repairing an electrical switch, my tame auto electrician gave the opinion that taking a switch apart was likely to result in odd bits falling out and falling apart. I thought I would test that hypothesis.

I bought a used switch from a specialist supplier. I plugged it in to see if it worked. It did. Now I knew that I had a backup in case anything dreadful happened when I took my faulty switch apart.

Rocker switches move

forwards/backwards and may have two or even three positions. Other versions, such as for window lifts, work against internal springs, so activate only when pushed.

Disconnect the faulty switch from its plug and wrap the plug with PVC tape. The plug pins are 'live' and should be protected from accidental contact with anything that might earth them. Take the switch inside, on a working tabletop that has plenty of light and no clutter.

Open up the faulty switch. You may lever off the button at the pivot pins with a plastic knife or edge. In any case, go gently lest you break something – the switch is invariably plastic. Be prepared for components to spring out when you open the housing. You don't want to do this in an untidy place where little widgets can get lost.

As I removed the button from the switch, my switch components stayed put, then simply tumbled out when I inverted the switch body. Study the internal layout and make notes or drawings before removing bits. A simplified diagram of what I found is shown here.

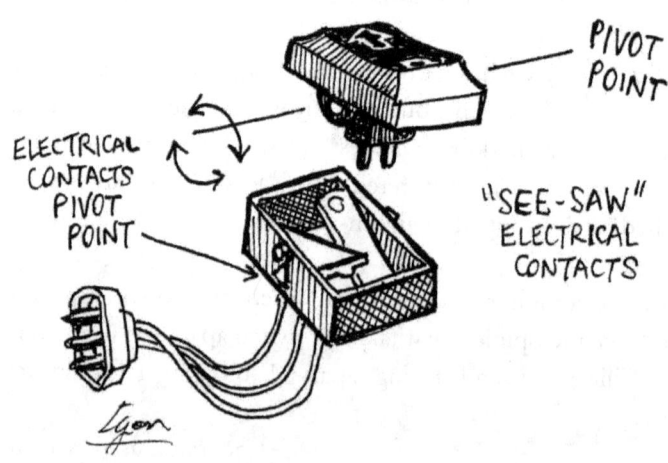

Basically, the window lift switch has a button which has a central pivot point. The base of the button has two spring-loaded 'legs'. These 'legs' push upon two electrical contacts made of copper. These contacts are strips of copper, stamped into peculiar but identical contours. They rest parallel to each other and can move like see-saws. These see-saws each have only one electrical contact that will go live, depending on which side the rocker button is pushed.

When the switch is pushed away from its neutral position to either one side or the other, the 'legs' of the button move in an arc and push against both copper strips. This pushes the contact of one strip onto a contact point in one corner of the switch body. The touching contacts close a circuit and current moves to activate the window lift motor. The other strip is also pushed against, but has no contact in its own corner. However, it has a contact on the other side. So when the switch is pushed the other way, that contact becomes live and the original contact is inactive.

This is a surprisingly simple and even elegant way of distributing electrical current in any of three possible positions. I was impressed by the simplicity.

Now why was the switch failing?

Basically, because the contacts were dirty. In fact, they looked black and 'burnt'. There was fine dust inside the switch housing and even a sliver of dried leaf fell out! It doesn't take much to stop a DC current of only 12 volts potential and this was more than enough. Hundreds of applications where electrical current passed through minute dust on the contacts had burnt the dust onto the metal surfaces, increasing resistance each time.

The answer was as simple as the design of the switch – clean the contacts!

I did this with an old toothbrush and detergent, scrubbing away at all the insides and surfaces. You can use methylated spirits for this cleaning if you want a faster drying time. I also used a spark plug / distributor points file to scrape away at all the contact surfaces. A simple metal nail file will do equally well here.

Once all the copper contacts are clean and shiny, oil them lightly with WD40 to protect the surfaces and ensure good electrical connectivity. Then replace the components and snap the button back on. The switch is ready to be re-installed, good as new. If you are doing extensive repairs or maintenance to your auto interior which involves removing and cleaning other parts, you could do worse than to take the opportunity and clean the insides of your rocker switches. Once you've done the first, the rest are easy.

There's one more problem you may have with your switch buttons that I will address here. That is the markings – or lack of them.

Buttons and switches are usually labelled directly with words or symbols on their surfaces. The very surface you push also identifies its function. Over time, these symbols or letters can wear away until they're gone.

Depending on the generation of vehicle you have, the imprint was either paint-stamped into the plastic surface or applied as a decal. The imprinted buttons can be easily cleaned and freshened with a toothbrush and detergent. Careful applications of white paint with fine model kit brushes can restore any missing fragments, provided that they can be masked with magic tape to make straight edges.

But once the decals are worn away, they're gone.

All the second-hand switches I found on offer had totally faded decal markings. Having paint-stamped switch buttons as a guide, I measured and recorded the dimensions of the figures. In my case, it was two arrows, one an outline the other a striped solid.

Next, I took out a sheet of decal stripes of various thicknesses. Made by Hasegawa for the kit modeller, the stripes (in white for this use) were divided into different widths, with sizes in 0.25, 050, 0.75 and 1.0 mm widths. I chose the correct thickness of stripe and began to cut out pieces in different lengths.

I applied these decal stripes virtually one by one, allowing some time for the previous stripe to dry. My best results were using the tip of a scalpel or toothpick to place each decal stripe on and manoeuvre it into place. Subsequent stripes must rest on top of previous ones. Use the tip of a tissue to absorb the water around the decal as soon as it's in position. This is a tedious evening's worth of work, but can be done while paying attention to TV or radio programs and even conversation, so it's not a total loss.

Depending on the complexity of the design you are reproducing and the patience and care you apply, your result will come up looking exactly like a factory original.

Letters and numbers are made from combinations of straight lines and curves. You can stick down straight line decals and carefully paint a curve between them to link them into one figure. For complex figures, you can cut a template from magic tape elsewhere and align it onto the button surface. When the masking is in place carefully paint it with as little paint on the hobby brush as possible. (Use an '00' or '000' size brush.) Peel off the magic tape when dry, then scrape off any excess paint with a scalpel tip or razor blade.

You can trim off excess lengths of decal stripes that stick out beyond the border of a figure with careful use of a scalpel or razor blade. You can also cut out and apply a solid decal and then remove pieces to arrive at the end result.

I used a combination of both for my window lift buttons. I built up my outline-only arrow figures with straight lengths of decal stripes of the same thickness. I made striped arrow figures by first cutting out the arrow in a solid decal and applying it to the button surface. Once dry, I used a scalpel and a metal rule. Using the rule as a straight-edge guide, I removed narrow strips from the decal. The result was a 'striped' arrow figure.

A better method is to find a good, clear reference for the figure or symbol you will need on the button. Scan this into a picture file at high resolution. Buy a sheet of transfer paper from a hobby outlet. This is a clear decal paper that can be printed on using your ink-jet printer at home.

You know where I'm going with this.

Take your image of the decal you want and size it according to the dimensions of your button's marking. Now tile the image on your file page so that you are placing several copies simultaneously onto the decal page. Print it out and you can cut out each symbol and apply the decal. You even have several spares for other buttons or in case of mistake.

You can even have a bit of fun with this and customise your buttons with unique images, symbols or words. Your friends will do a double-take when they see personalised buttons and switchgear – particularly if they look 'factory stock'. (But don't make it so obscure that no one else will be able to drive it!)

For a little more effort, you can make an entire transfer sheet of multiple figures for buttons and switches to suit a particular make and model of car or truck. If there's demand from the collector or car club community for reproductions, you've got yourself a small business! Advertise in club publications or club web sites for low fees or for free if you're a member. You could even build an international clientele – decal sheets you print off (and an instruction sheet you make up) can be posted like letters all round the world.

How's that for a great niche business idea? Just say you saw it here first!

Once the transfers have been applied to your buttons and are dry, you will need to protect them from wearing away from all those applications of fingertips. This will involve applying a couple of clear coats of enamel or lacquer.

The methods I've described here take more care than skill. Basically, anyone can repair and refinish rocker switches. Women readers – if you've ever painted a nail or repaired a broken one, you can do all this too.

A clear gloss enamel can be chosen if all the buttons are shiny. A matt finish could be closer to the look you need to match. Most buttons may well be somewhere in between – a satin finish. A little tin of clear satin varnish can be purchased from a hobby store – it's only a couple of dollars and the small amount is about all you will need.

When dry, re-install the buttons and attach to the wiring plugs. Once surrounding panels are in place, you will be surprised at how freshened the controls look with clear, bold, function markings once more.

Interior Repairs - VW Golf Hatchback Cover

There are many ways to effect repairs to your interior without resorting to replacement parts or professional help. I'll give one example.

As mentioned previously, the first car of my own was a 1976 VW Golf 3-door hatchback. It was an efficient design but suffered from some poor materials and features in its Australian-assembled version.

Beneath the hatchback door was a luggage cover panel that raised and lowered with it. This lid hid the boot (or trunk) and its contents from prying sunlight and prying eyes. It was made of some kind of cross between cardboard and chipboard. I imagine this mulch-pulp being made through a process of mastication by a cow, kept on a pasture behind the car factory.

Needless to say, when I bought the car it was only five years old and already the luggage cover had deteriorated to the point that it would fall into the trunk itself. The edges on the sides had crumbled away. They would no longer hold the cover panel on the supports provided by small fixed panels on each side.

The solution was to reinforce these edges with something more durable. I bought a length of aluminium angle from a hardware store - the normal right-angle extrusion. Then I measured it and cut it by handsaw into two pieces. A test fit confirmed that the boot cover panel would rest on its side supports by using the horizontal surfaces of the aluminium angles.

Now I needed to find a way to attach the aluminium angles to the flaky, crumbling boot cover. The solution was to sandwich it. I would clamp the panel between the aluminium angle piece and a sheet of tinned metal.

I measured and cut two strips of tinned metal with snips. Next I measured out and drilled a number of evenly spaced holes in the angle and matching holes in the tin sheet. The holes were to accommodate pop rivets, but a nut and bolt with split washer will do equally well.

I used a pop rivet gun and inserted the rivets so that they held the tin sheet strip and aluminium angle together, with the boot cover panel between them. The tin metal formed a firm backing for the rivets. I did each side and test fitted my newly repaired panel.

Perfect! The new sides were parallel and accurate. Not only was the panel repaired but strengthened as well – in all likelihood, the edges would outlast the car itself. The extra weight of the metal was minimal and the hydraulic hatchback struts lifted both the hatchback and luggage cover as before, with no problems.

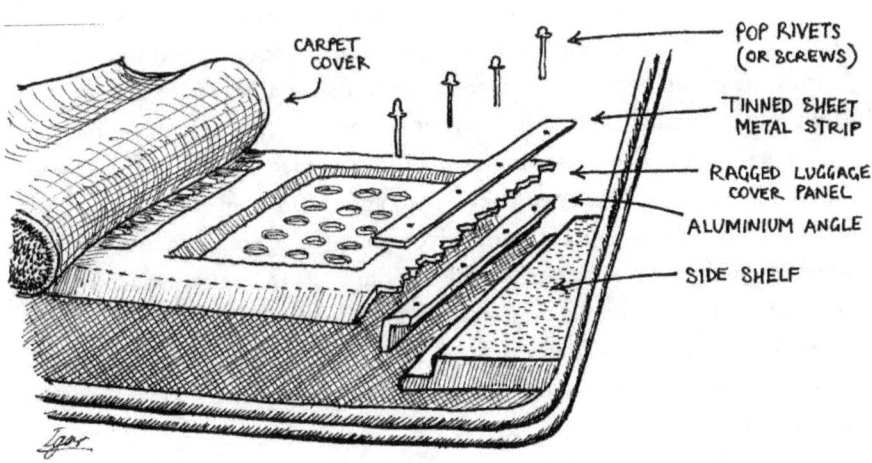

The luggage cover panel was lined with a rather cheap and nasty black carpet on top. It was simply attached with spray adhesive by the factory and the adhesive had perished long before. I had the option of returning the carpet to the cover panel with spray adhesive or replacing it with a higher quality auto floor carpet. I did the latter. A simple offcut of black carpet from an auto upholsterer's was all that was required. It was measured and cut with carpet or thick cloth scissors, with some overlap allowed for. Once in place, spray adhesive was used in lieu of something more ambitious, and the finer black carpet was in place. Its deeper pile and thicker body gave a more luxurious feel to the rear than the factory had ever produced. It also insulated against noise.

Is it Heightened Reality? Or just doing as the factory should have done to begin with?

So, are there ragged internal panels in your trunk or interior that could do with some strengthening or repair?

Brushed Aluminium or Stainless Steel Finish?

Some auto manufacturers wanted a brushed stainless steel appearance to highlight their interiors. But they were too cheap to use these materials, so they substituted silver painted plastic with a vaguely 'brushed' look. My VW Golf was a case in point.

We can do better.

Use a similar approach to wood-graining as described below. Have a sample of brushed stainless steel or aluminium to look at and to compare with your result. If you wish to create or re-create a brushed stainless steel trim finish on what is basically a plastic surface, follow these directions.

It is recommended that you detach the trim piece so that you can work on it on a table top. You need good light and room to move.

Choose either a spraycan of silver paint or a spraycan of 'chrome' paint. You'll never get a chrome plated finish from a spraycan, but that's not the intention here. You will obtain a more silvery silver, as the 'chrome' spray paint is loaded with extra metal flakes. Brushing on silver is not recommended, as it is difficult to smooth out streaks, and you need an even base to start from.

Spray on the silver paint and set aside to dry.

When it's thoroughly dry, follow up with a fine 1200 grit sandpaper. Rub lightly with a straight, continuous movement, from one end to the other. Unlike woodgraining (described elsewhere) where you recreate fractal, chaotic textures of nature, with brushed stainless steel you are mimicking the hard-edged, straight lines of artificial finishes. In some ways, this is more difficult. You must resist the tendency to move your arm in an arc – you are reproducing a straight, machine-made 'brushing'.

Use a light touch. Subtle is the goal here, not overt. Too heavy a 'brushed' sanding will just look like what it is – a lot of scratches in silver paint. Check regularly with the texture of the trim or sample you want to duplicate.

Once again, it's recommended that you try this out on some scrap pieces first, before committing to your actual trim.

It's highlights like timber veneer or brushed stainless steel that really bring a touch of class to an automotive interior. They catch the light or give off a warm glow. Give the automobile stylists their due and restore these features to make your interior look factory-fresh.

New Contours for Old Seats

Bucket seats look great when they're doing the bucket thing and holding your behind in place. Over time, the plastic foam that they're padded with will lose its resiliency and crush. This will make for a flat seat surface which no longer does the bucket thing and may even be less comfortable.

You can renew your seats by cutting strips of plastic foam and insert them on top of the existing foam padding. Use a spray adhesive to keep the added layer in place. The perfect opportunity is when you are re-upholstering your seats. You can work with a professional upholsterer or do it yourself if you have bought a new seat 'skin'. Most seat covers are attached to the seat frame with little metal hooks or circlets around the perimeter of the 'skin'. Use needle-nose pliers to open up these hooks just enough to work free from the perimeter frame. Be careful not to tear the cloth or vinyl that the seat 'skin' is made from.

If you have access to the seat frame and springs, take the opportunity to wipe them clean and apply either WD40 or a fish oil or other treatment for surface rust. Lay lots of newspaper underneath to stop any drips onto carpet.

During your experimentation, you can re-attach the seat skin temporarily by bending closed a couple of hooks. When you're satisfied with your new seat contours, align the cover carefully and close the hooks or circlets around the frame perimeter.

If only it was this easy to reshape yourself into a Brad Pitt or an Angelina Jolie!

Floor Foundations and Carpeting Capers

If you've done some extensive internal restoration involving removing the seats and centre console, you can take this opportunity to ensure that all the metal of the floor pan is clean and free from any rust.

You can also inspect the electrical wiring routed along a side sill, checking it for frayed insulation on the wires and do some repairs and trouble-shooting here. You can also lay down extra cables for speakers which you will install and connect later. Finally, you can encase your wires in a conduit for future scuff protection. Tape it down as flat as you can to avoid carpet distortions. Use a duct tape or preferably a high-temperature duct tape which will remain sticky if heated by the proximity of exhaust pipe heat underneath.

Last but not least, you can renew the carpet!

If it is torn or worn in places, it should be renewed. A variety of moulded carpets are available for various models, and chances are good that you can source a new one this way.

However, this is not always the case and you may have better luck sourcing a good carpet set from the junkyard or wrecker's. (See 'Spare Parts – Hunting and Gathering' below.) Black is fairly easy to find a match for but certain colours may be harder. Look for integrity of pile, particularly in high-use areas, such as under the driver's feet. A little mud from other people's footprints at the yard is not as important as the lack of wear on the pile and whether the colour has not faded anywhere.

A spare heel pad could be found if your original is torn. Remove the carpet as a unit, taking care not to damage any mounting brackets at the edges. Keep all the fasteners used to hold down the carpet set, even if you have a complete set on your vehicle. Plastic fasteners can break with little warning and having a few spares is always good insurance. As always, bag 'em and tag 'em.

Often the underlay beneath the carpet is undamaged and usable as is but sometimes it may have been flooded. If it's a jute felt, it will just fall apart. Cotton waste from the clothing industry was a popular underlay material – it was unwanted and cheap. A replacement could be sourced with the carpet at a wrecker's or you could spend a little more and buy a modern upgrade. This could be a felt, or a more advanced sandwich underlay, consisting of a high density bitumen centre sheet between a layer of felt on the outsides.

A step above this again is a product from Germany called Resomat®. This is a sheet underlay which includes a layer of aluminium foil. It is superior to bitumen- or PVC-based underlays in that it won't outgas. It's also more effective as an acoustic barrier by absorbing metal drumming or vibrations in the floor panels of the vehicle. As a bonus, it has a self-adhesive backing for easier fitting. This underlay is claimed to be installed in the Queen of England's Bentley and in the president of the United States' Cadillac. If it's good enough for the Prez, it's probably good enough for you too.

When installing the underlay liner directly on the metal, press it down and flatten overlap areas as much as you can. Before installing your carpet, you may wish to tailor the fit a bit better around the sides of the driveshaft tunnel. An extra strip of underlay padding here and there may serve to ease a carpet contour to prevent an unnecessary fold or creasing. An uneven floor pressing may need an extra layer of underfelt to arrive at a flat surface. When the carpet is laid over this, the effect fill be much neater.

Trim the underlay clear of the door sills area to allow the step plates to sit flat and even as before.

Lay the carpet out and press it in place, working from the centre outwards to the corners. Most interior carpets come in two halves – front and rear. This makes it easier to ensure a good fit. Install the appropriate fasteners as you go.

You can borrow a hair dryer (or use your own of course) and heat up a section of carpet that you want to form into a difficult corner. Position the dryer about 12" (or 30cm) from the carpet. Hold the carpet in place with your other hand while using the hair dryer. When the hand on the carpet is uncomfortable hot (not blistered!) you know that the carpet's plastic backing has softened sufficiently to gently stretch and form into that corner or edge.

Creases in the carpet can be treated with a hair dryer and a weight such as a stone or block of metal. (Make sure the weight is clean!) Work your way out towards an edge, about one or two inches (25-50mm) at a time. You can also use the heel of your hand or your foot as a press, wherever it's easier.

If you are using a new moulded carpet, there may be variations in controls or fittings that are not allowed for by the after-market supplier. Where you need to create a hole in the carpet, use a Stanley blade or sharp knife and slice an 'X' there. Start with a small incision and test fit. It is easier to enlarge it than it is to try and gather up the edges of too big a hole.

Find the seat attachment bolts on the floor and make small cuts in the carpet to allow them to emerge. Any sharp tool can be used to feel for the holes of nuts recessed into the floor. Make a mark with chalk and return with a sewing needle or similar to poke a fine hole in the carpet backing. Be sure to wipe the needle clean before returning it to your wife's sewing basket!

If there is an excess of carpet where it meets the front kick panels, allow a slight overlap. When test fitting the kick panel, it should rest over the carpet without a visible gap between the panel and carpet edge.

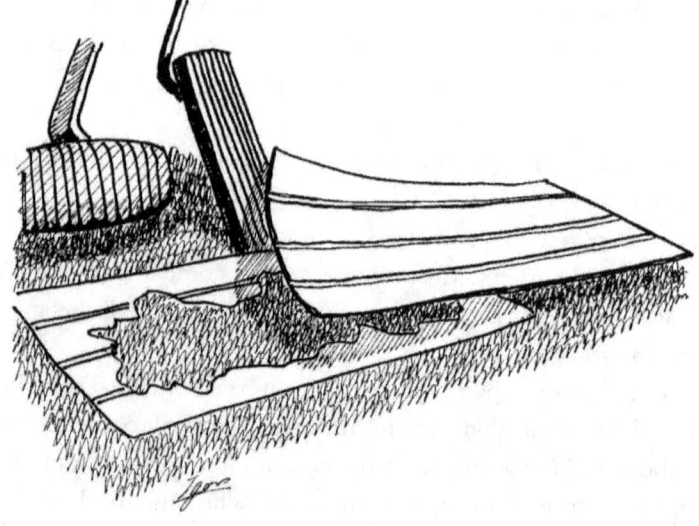

If you have an excess of carpet after a fairly good fitting-in, it is best to push it together in a gathering under the centre console. With the console assembly in place, the gathering will be unseen.

Allow some carpet excess to extend under the step plates at your door sills. Ensure the plate bolt holes are repeated in the carpet underneath.

If you are replacing the heel pad on a second-hand carpet, it may be easiest to retain the scraps of the old one in place. Then simply glue the new pad to the remnants of the old. You can align them accurately and a good epoxy glue will hold it firm when set. A vinyl-to-vinyl bond is simpler to achieve than a vinyl-to-carpet adhesion. Leave it to dry before disturbing it!

The final result will be a quieter cabin which will mean more restful travel on long trips and more nuance in the music you hear. Or your music tastes may require no nuances at all, in which case you will be looking to put a sub-woofer in somewhere!

Like wearing a well-tailored dress or suit, a well-tailored car interior will bring pride and satisfaction. Doesn't it feel good (after your attention to detail) to have taken a Wal-Mart interior and improved it to an Armani?

General Interior Cleaning

Vacuum the carpets and cloth seats and cloth roof lining if fitted. This will usually raise a bit of dust which settles out, so do this first.

Then wipe the surfaces. Generally, most vinyls, plastics and leatherettes and even leathers need only a moist cloth or chamois to clean and wipe down. Modest amounts of liquid soap or detergent can be used. Bear in mind that some detergents will attack plastics, so read the label first.

Finish off with a clean cloth and a protectant dressing, like 303 Vinyl Protectant.

Clean the inside of all the glass, particularly the windscreen. Annoying finger marks or other smears need to be wiped into history.

Spray some silicon lubricant or even squirt some drops of engine oil into the felt lined channels that your windows travel up and down in. Whether they are manual or power windows, you may be amazed at the extra ease with which they raise and lower.

Deflector Screens Against Death Rays

Windshield reflector sheets can serve to save your new interior or prevent the rapid deterioration of your old one. They're a thin plastic sheet coated on one side with a silvery foil. Reflectors are folded up like a map and when unfolded attach with little straps to sun visors or other protrusions.

These shades / reflectors are cheap and several can be used behind your windscreen and back window, or set up along the side – anywhere where you anticipate lots of sun while your car is parked. Your vehicle cabin has enough glass to be a greenhouse. You want to make it more like a covered tent.

By mounting reflector sheets close to the glass windows, they will prevent direct infra-red rays from hitting and heating up your interior surfaces by reflecting those rays back out. The build-up of ambient heat in your interior will be lessened and plastic substances within will be protected from excessive temperatures that cause outgassing.

PART 3. INTERIOR WARMTH THROUGH WONDERFUL WOODWORK

Creative Woodgraining

Driving a car is a sensual experience. Sure, there's a feeling of power and freedom, however spurious. What is felt immediately, though, by both driver and passengers, is how it feels to sit inside a car. The softness of the seat cushioning, the coolness or warmth of upholstered surfaces on bare skin, the feel of switches and controls, even the scent of the interior.

Car manufacturers pay attention to these things, today more than ever. The tactile 'feel' of a switch is an extra consideration above the reliability of the switch operation. Seat surfaces, their contours, level of lumbar support and adjustability rank high in the science of ergonomics.

Beyond the science though, is the art of making a person feel comfortable in an automotive interior. This is where a degree of luxury or perceived luxury is adopted in design and manufacture.

One example of luxurious appointment is with leather seating. Excellent vinyls and leatherettes have been offered that are all but indistinguishable from cowhide, yet real leather still commands added appreciation and value.

Another example is interior woodwork. Inlays of timber, rich in fine grains and colours lend a warmth and undeniable feeling of luxury to any automotive interior in a way that plastics, vinyls and even cloths cannot. Even fake timber inlays made from plastics can also impart this look and feeling.

A brief history of wood trim will put things in context here. The earliest motor vehicles used timber framed bodies. Sometimes an exposed timber surface, such as a dashboard, was simply varnished rather than painted. This showed off the quality and grain of the wood which set off the handful of brass gauges and instruments nicely.

By the time mass production was adopted, decorative wood was largely forgotten. Pressed metal panels and yards of cloth or leather were the only viable answers to mass produced interiors. The only exceptions were the custom-built bodies specified by wealthy automobile buyers.

The 1930s was a revolutionary time for car design and mass production methods. Pressures on manufacturers to build more for less were immense. The variety of models offered was cut, prices were slashed and designs modernised and streamlined year by year. Engineers were extorted to find new processes that would simplify manufacture and still produce an acceptable automobile.

The timber graining on this 1937 Buick dashboard is typical of the Thirties. The grain went vertically on windscreen garnish mouldings but horizontally across dashboard surfaces. Notice the patterns continuing unbroken across the glove box lid.

By the mid-1930s, a new fashion was bringing luxury – or the look of it – to American car interiors. This was the use of wood-graining on metal surfaces such as the dashboard, interior door cappings and inside window surrounds. The effect was surprisingly realistic and much more durable than real wood inserts. It brought a rich, warm ambience to an auto interior, something that the comfortable but drab cloth upholsteries of the time could not do. And as an important bonus, wood-graining was a great deal cheaper than real wood, especially for a mass-produced car.

This dashboard is from a 1942 Pontiac Torpedo Eight. Though the wood finish looks rich and exotic, it's only painted steel. Choose your reference material well before attempting patterns this complex.

Expert craftsmen would use sponges rather than brushes to recreate exotic and beautiful timber veneers, based on timbers like walnut, maple and so on. With a bit of practice, you too can learn from these craftsmen and their methods.

Observe the fine, dense wood-grain simulation on this 1940 Dodge coupe. The whole dashboard and windscreen reveal mouldings are the work of an artisan's hand.

A simpler woodgrain spans this 1946 Oldsmobile dashboard, offsetting the generous chrome trim. It is best to remove obstructing assemblies so they won't interfere with the graining process. He's more thrilled with his Hydra-Matic transmission than with his woodgrained dashboard, which was very conventional by 1946.

These wood-graining methods continued into the 1940s, and were gradually dropped for new styling trends in the Fifties. By the early Sixties, however, fashions had swung back again to the distinctive look of wood veneer accents in car interiors. And the Seventies saw an explosion of plastic and vinyl woodgrain accents everywhere – on dashboards, consoles, steering wheels, doors and even outside!

Some manufacturers, like Studebaker, were on a severe budget. Their 1963-4 woodgrained dashboards were a simple flat brown colour with an overlay of black, dot-screen print, in a veneer pattern. The illusion was quite realistic, at least before the colour faded. Other makers used the new plastic, simulated timber inserts that looked authentic and were, of course, still considerably cheaper than the real thing.

The use of real timber pieces or veneers was common among the higher-priced English and European cars, but also made a modest appearance from Detroit. Chrysler's 1965 Imperial brochure boasted of 'inlays of rare 100-year-old walnut… out of each 52 ½ lbs. of harvested claro walnut, we can find only 8 oz. fit for Imperial.' This particular walnut was found growing in only two places on Earth – and this was in 1965!

By 1971, woodgraining was returning to many automobile interiors, even certain models of the Low Price Three. This Plymouth GTX or Road Runner instrument binnacle has a sculpted plastic inlay. Even the steering wheel rim is woodgrained!

You won't find anything rare in a production car today, even in an expensive one. The fact is, rare timbers are getting rarer. This is due to destructive farming and logging practices that are destroying rainforests at an alarming rate. Can you imagine the heat that Mercedes-Benz would cop from the German Greens if it was caught using destructively harvested timber for their luxury wood interior pieces?

So do your bit and save the planet – substitute real paint for real wood!

If you have an interior you wish to restore where timber inlays – whether real of fake – are looking drab or muddy, it's essential to bring them back to new condition. Otherwise all your other good work may be undermined.

It's obvious that the metal surfaces found in car and truck interiors from the 1930s can be renewed with wood graining. Also the plastic wood grains from the 1960s and 1970s that may have worn or faded with decades of use.

With the extensive after-market industries in new parts for muscle cars and the like, specific decals for some of these veneers may be available. Or if you're less lucky, these timber accents can be renewed with your own paint, skill and effort.

Firstly, research your subject. Go to your local library for close-up detailed and preferably coloured pictures of woodgrain of various trees. You might start with walnut, a fairly common wood used in English cars over the years.

Are you recreating the factory look or going mild custom? You might even consider exotic timbers like zebra wood, which looks exactly as you would expect it to, (just a bit browner).

Internet search engines might deliver excellent examples of woodgrain images, moreover, you can download them and print them to scale, so that you have the right patterns to copy.

Remember, you're dealing with the fractal geometry of nature. You want something *like, not exactly like*. You want the feel of that kind of timber grain, whether it is the graining texture or the mixture of colours and shades, even occasional knot-holes.

The warmth of a walnut timber without the cost. Even for this posh 1969 Ford Thunderbird Landau, it was acceptable to substitute a plastic or vinyl veneer or even a decal for the real thing. This piece would be easily removable if it had to be wood-grained, and the simple graining just as easy to reproduce. Note the fussy grain highlight in the steering wheel hub.

Creating the Fake Timber Inlay

If the piece you want to do is removable easily, by all means remove it to help you either paint it or if it's too delicate or gone, to make a replica of it.

Some veneer strips for furniture edges are made that come with an adhesive so that they can be 'ironed' on to a piece of furniture. They come in useful strips, ready to unroll and cut to size. If you find a veneer pleasing to your taste, then, you're almost finished. Just cut it to size and iron it on.

The alternative is to recreate the fake timber trim with sheets of plastic or - surprise – even wood. Usually thin plywood.

Or from sheet metal, if that is the era of your car or truck. There may be safety concerns if you wish to use metal panels on a dashboard with an air bag behind it. Use your common sense! Pick only the base materials appropriate to your era of car or truck.

Accurately measure the piece you want to duplicate. Make a template out of cardboard, or even paper to start with, so as to get an accurate outline. Then use this template to make another template. Check always to ensure that mistakes in measurement and fabrication don't creep in.

Most wood veneer pieces are rectangular. Ensure that the corners are not sharp. You won't find any sharp corners in a car interior. Carefully round the corners off slightly, and do all of them evenly. Rounded corners are less likely to snag and tear clothing or to become damaged if a corner is lifted or snapped off after such a snag.

Make some test pieces, preferably from the same material you will be wood-graining for your auto interior. Clean them with detergent to remove any grease or oils from your hands, and dry thoroughly. Use these test pieces and PRACTISE FIRST. This is a new skill you are learning and you will make mistakes. Make them on things you can throw away.

Based on the type of timber grain you wish to recreate, choose your brown enamel paints. There are various browns, some yellowish, some very red, some almost khaki. Examine the lightest and darkest shades of the wood you want to reproduce. Isolate them and see if you can buy or mix those shades. Be aware of the colour balance you are after, too. A paint shop could custom mix small pots of paint for you, or you could find approximations off-the-shelf. Choose two or even three brown enamels to give you some range.

Car wash sponges can break apart into small pieces. Shout yourself a new sponge and tear apart the old sponge into small pieces. These should be no bigger than the palm of your hand. Remember, you're wood-graining small areas. (If you're doing a whole dashboard from the 1930s-1940s, larger sponges are a good idea but no bigger than the span of your hand.)

Open and stir your brown enamel paints. Pour out a small amount from each onto clean surfaces you can use as paint palettes. Though you should start with the paler brown you have chosen and add on the darker shade, you will still be applying at least two different browns at the same time, while both are still wet. Use a unique sponge for each colour.

Have an extra sponge, kept moist (not wet) with turpentine. (Warning: turps attacks plastics. Test your use of it on scrap first.)

If you're using acrylics (water-based paints) you can apply the paint on any substance that is not absorbent. Ensure that the paint is meant for interior/exterior use, as the heat build-up and sunlight inside the car can test a purely indoors paint.

Load a small amount of paint from one palette onto a piece of sponge. The paint is 'dry', meaning it is not thinned with solvent. Apply it to your surface in an even line. But not too even – streaks in timber grain weave around knot holes, change thickness, even stop and start. You're not covering a surface with paint – you're streaking it.

Move right across from one end to the other. Once done, try the other brown. Streak it across. Change the pressure of your hand upon the surface to change the thickness of the streaks. Subtly twist and roll your piece of sponge. Use the roughness of your applicator itself to ensure that you are not laying on too even a streak.

If you've dripped a blob of paint, streak it out. If it's too big to smear out, use your sponge with solvent (turps for enamel, water for acrylic) and lightly wipe it off. If your graining is becoming too dark or acquiring the wrong texture, you can remove some of what you have applied while it's still wet. Think of it as an 'undo' function on your computer. Bear in mind though, that like with your computer, you can really only undo the last few steps.

To reproduce some of those strange, whorled wood-grain accents that seemed to be favoured in the early Seventies, you may need to dab with your sponges, rather than streaking them. Even applying your paint in a *twisting* motion may be useful. Test on scrap first to get the right effects.

Clean your sponge applicators occasionally to stop them from becoming clogged and solid with drying paint. Be sure to squeeze out all the solvent before using the sponges. They should be moist with solvent, not wet.

Get the feel of your tools and materials. Always refer back to your visual references. Only when you're confident with your results can you attempt to create the real veneer. (Have a duplicate original piece so that you can pick the best of two.)

Always work on a table top. Avoid doing it *in situ* in the car, such as on the dashboard. There's not enough room to move in the car; it's awkward to reach from desired angles; and it's not well ventilated enough. There's also the possibility of paint spills onto the seats, carpet, dashboard or other surfaces. The difficulty of the clean-up after such an accident doesn't bear even thinking about.

Once you have covered the underlying surface with an appropriate density of colour, you can concentrate your technique on achieving the right balance of shades and wood-grain.

When you've finished, take the piece(s) to a place where they can dry. This should preferably be where they will not attract dust. Indoors is good. If you can do so without spoiling the paint, rest the piece(s) upside down.

Once dry, take them to your vehicle and hold them roughly where they'll go in your dashboard or interior. Do they look like you expected? Is it different? Are you happy with it? How does it look in full sunlight and in shade?

Ask your friends if the finished piece looks good. 'Yes men' are of no use here, nor are the destructive criticisers. You want honest opinions, or none at all.

If you're unhappy with your first finished attempt, you can start over, frequently on the same insert panel. Use a solvent to clean off the paint and you're ready to start again. Of course, it's better to gain experience on your practice pieces first.

If you're happy with the result, move on to make another piece.

When two pieces will be adjacent to each other, such as across a dashboard or side-by-side door cappings, try to obtain a similarity of timber grain and colour, as if they were harvested from the same tree. If, for example, you have a veneer dashboard which surrounds a glovebox door, assemble the panels on your work table exactly as they will appear when mounted in place. Wood-grain them together, so that all your streaks will match as they cross the gap from one panel to the other. Rolls-Royce craftsmen always seek to match the shade and character of real timber veneers where they will be assembled side by side. You could do worse than to follow their example.

When you have completed the wood-graining of all the parts, protect them with a clear finish, perhaps more than one coat of it. If you want a completely smooth finish, spray it on.

But beware! I have seen and touched some real timber inlays whose surfaces were so smooth and polished, that they felt like plastic – and looked it.

There's something to be said for a more tactile effect to wood finishes. If you're thinking of the texture of a grained timber, then apply your clear lacquer with a brush, in the same direction as the grain. A sympathetic approach here will create a wooden texture, as if the wood has not been completely smothered in layers of polished clear coats.

Beware of loose brush bristles – remove them immediately. Use a good quality brush that won't lose its bristles so easily. You can't scrimp here!

And remember - always use the same solvent base for your clear coat as you used for the underlying paint. If they're different, the solvent may attack the paint beneath and ruin your wood impression.

Real Woodgraining - Restoring Real Wood

Where a quote for removal and re-fitting of wood veneers for a classic car (and the stripping, staining and lacquering that comes in-between) might run into thousands, there's really no alternative but to do it yourself.

Approach local carpenters or wood workers at local craft fairs and the like. Talk to retired, hobby woodworkers also. You might be able to do a deal with them, and as they don't have commercial overheads, they may be able to do just as good a job for a fraction of the price. They're also good for advice or minor piece work you can't do yourself.

There are several things to aim for in a complete refurbishing of the

wood veneer:
1. A flat finish, smooth as glass;
2. A clear, transparent finish;
3. A re-colouring of the stain that's faithful to the original;
4. A finish that's resistant to ultraviolet light;
5. An invisible repair of any breaks in the veneer.

Which Finish?

That's the question. There are a number of alternatives, each with its pros and cons.

Acrylic Lacquer is an excellent choice. This automotive topcoat has several advantages:
1. It dries quickly, therefore there's less likelihood of contamination with dust;
2. It gives a hard, durable finish, like glass;
3. It's flexible enough to resist damage from the expansion and contraction caused by a wide range of ambient temperatures. Therefore, it won't craze or delaminate.
4. It's proven to resist the ravages of ultraviolet light.

Spar Varnish is a good alternative. It's an oil-based varnish that's a long chain molecule. Say what? Briefly, long chain molecules indicate a substance that's more fragile and prone to breakage than short-chain molecules.

Spar varnish is stable and flexible – it won't delaminate like other finishes.

On the other hand:
1. The linseed oil that it's based on darkens with ultraviolet exposure over time;
2. Polish doesn't take as well;
3. The finish is soft and will mark easily;
4. It dries slowly, causing risk of contamination with dust;
5. To avoid this risk, metallic salts are used to speed up the drying process. These salts attack the finish in turn, and are toxic to handle.

Varnish (the short chain molecule version, take note) is a good choice with the finish. However:

1. It's brittle, with no flexibility to accommodate variations in temperature and humidity. Varnish will crack and craze.
2. When applied commercially for the car maker, varnish finishes were quick dried with metallic salts. This leaves them even more prone to cracking.

Two-Pack Urethane is a relative newcomer to the wood finish world. It gets kudos for giving an extremely hard and durable finish with excellent surface and clarity.

Unfortunately:

1. It's cyanide based and therefore toxic;
2. It sets hard, as it's an epoxy. So hard that there may be clean-up problems.
3. It's also so hard that if it's damaged, it may be a problem to remove without damaging the underlying timber veneer.
4. It might delaminate over time. This has the appearance of a milky finish.

Single-Pack Urethane. Is it half the value of a two-pack? No, in fact it gives a hard surface and good finish, just not as incredibly hard as the two-pack.

But:

1. If it gets struck or knocked, single pack urethane will delaminate, leaving small milky marks.
2. If a sealing coat is not applied, the urethane will delaminate over time, with the clear finish becoming more opaque. Oww!

Nitro-Cellulose Lacquer is still around, but it's extremely old technology and hard to find these days. No wonder – though it gives a good finish, it's brittle and will crack and craze.

Shellac – that wonder domestic substance of the 1920s and 1930s – could be painted over surfaces to give them a coating of glamour. Used extensively by Hollywood movie set builders, shellac gave a clear, glossy finish and was made from – believe it or not – ground-up insect body casings. Therefore the name – 'shell-ac'.

Shellac gives a wonderful finish, being the basis for the fine craft of French polishing.

No longer welcome though, are such features as:
1. It won't take getting wet. Water will produce white marks.
2. Shellac is brittle and damages easily – impact chips show.
3. It is also damaged by methylated spirits. So you can't clean anything nearby with this solvent.

Various oils and waxes are left over to consider for timber veneer, some of which have been used for centuries. They give an excellent finish and soft wood patina, but:
1. Do not physically protect the wood from wear or scuffing;
2. Do not protect the wood from water damage;
3. Require frequent re-application to maintain the finish.

There are a couple of basic things to avoid.

Firstly, if you want a satin finish, never use an out-of-the-can satin spray. Some products are made with finely crushed quartz to arrive at the satin finish. This powder attacks the resistance to ultraviolet light damage and increases the brittleness of the finish. That's not listed on the can now is it?

It is better to use a gloss finish and then to rub it down to satin with a 1000 grit wet-and-dry sandpaper or a compound polish cream.

Incidentally, the metallic look that's given to personal care products such as shampoos and hair conditioners is caused by the use of finely crushed fish scales. That nice, silky hair conditioner is based on pig fat. Waste not, want not.

Secondly, avoid mixing your products on your wood veneer. For example, do not cover an acrylic lacquer with a urethane, or vice versa. They will 'fight' and over the long term, will exfoliate. That's something you want your skin to do, not your timber veneer. Your finish will start to peel off within a few years.

Now to the work.

Repairing Timber Veneer

The wood veneer tends to be damaged most on the edges, where small chunks may be chipped off. Fortunately, this is also easiest to fix. A spare veneer from a sacrificial or donor piece is required to fill the gaps, so to speak. This can come from a leftover piece or a closely matched veneer with the right grain and colour. Sometimes, a small chunk can be removed from the rear of a door capping or other piece as long as it's out of sight from all angles.

To repair the veneer, the base material needs to be stabilised to prevent further splintering or damage. An application of 5 minute Araldite or similar glue is good for this purpose.

Clean up the edges with a sharp Stanley knife or similar blade. Glue on the donor piece, which you have cut to fit into the gap in the veneer. Be careful to line up the grain of the veneer with the piece you are applying. Use a jeweller's or watch-maker's eye-piece to check this out in detail.

Make sure your replacement piece is longer so that it overlaps where the edge of the wood capping is. This way, when the glue dries, you can cut the excess overhang off. Do the overhang cutting off from behind, not from the front backwards. Use the edge of the wood as a cutting guide.

If there are large areas of damage, repair them in small sections at a time. Start with the most unobtrusive spots, then as your skill improves, move on.

Stripping the Old Finish

The old varnish must first be stripped and sanded off. You can use a fruit knife or similar edged implement to scrape it off. Be careful not to press too hard and dig into the wood. You are just lightly scraping the surface.

A citrus-based paint stripper can be used as it is the least chemically intrusive on the timber, but do all you can with 'mechanical' varnish removal first. It's better to scrape it all off than to use 'product'.

Once it is mostly off, finish with a light sanding of 400 grit dry paper. Important things to avoid when sanding are the metal wool scourers. If you use a steel wool in wet sanding, you may leave rust marks in your wood grain.

If you use a stainless steel wool, you won't leave rust marks, but you may leave score marks in the wood that would be difficult to mend, without a great deal of sanding down, or not at all.

Leave the steel scourers to the rough, heavy chassis work underneath the car.

Types of Stain

There are two basic types of stain – there is a surface stain with the highest optical clarity, meaning it's the most transparent. This type is preferred.

The other type is a particulate suspension stain which is more stable under UV light but it ends up in a brown, almost muddy colour.

Lesser quality timber veneers are often stained to give them a depth of colour obtainable only with rare or hard to find timbers. Stains can also be selectively applied to the darker streaks of the grain with a fine brush. This is to bring out the rich detail found in some timber grain. It can be easy to overdo the dark streaks with stain. We won't consider this method, as it requires some judgment and experience with this type of work.

Apply the surface stain with a rag only. Soak the stain onto the rag, then apply the rag to the wood. Rub the stain in. Do not apply the stain directly to the wood, as it may soak in more in one patch than another. You may be left with a blotchy colour effect that's difficult to fix. The wood is fibrous after all and will soak up oils or liquids. Apply the stain evenly.

The British did it best. This 1950s Jaguar XK120 convertible coupe is loaded with real, chunky timber pieces, exquisitely fitted and finished. It's better to keep this maintained, but if not, to be restored piece by piece.

Applying a Lacquer Spray

Once the stain is dry and even it's time to cover it with our chosen protective lacquer.

Apply the base coat and when dry, wet sand it with 400 grit paper.

Finish with the sealer coat. This should be a half/half mixture of solvent and paint. You can adjust this if you are using an air brush. If you are using a spray can, apply a thin coat.

There is usually a four hour wait between sprayed coats. Repeat the coats and don't be disappointed if you have a dull, flat finish. This is normal.

You want to apply repeated coats to give a decent coating. Do not apply any thick coats. Make them all thin. You can't save time here. You're already saving money by doing it yourself. About 8 to 10 coats are sufficient.

You will know you're done when only about 2% of the low points in the wood surface show in the lacquer. That is, you've filled up most of the grain, but not all. These valleys will disappear at the last polishing stage.

An important thing to remember is to always leave an area of the wood in the raw state exposed to the air. Of course, this is the back side of your door capping or trim piece, where it is unseen. The reason s so that the wood can dry if it becomes wet. Moisture can find its way into wood through capillary action and there needs to be a path for the moisture to escape. If most of the wood surface is sealed, then the moisture will be trapped inside. With the heat of a car interior on a hot day, the combination will cook the wood! This is the royal road to wood rot.

SEAL COAT

The First Seal Coat: The Lacquer Coat

The first step is to use a machine compound paste to polish the lacquer surface. Jeweller's rouge is the best type. The result should be a satin finish or old style patina.

Next, use a slurry of diatomaceous earth and a very fine, 2000 grit wet n' dry sandpaper. This will give you that glass-like finish.

Some points to remember are to apply this in small patches, roughly the size of a large coin. Use a linen tea towel to trap the slurry. Rub until the slurry loses its watery nature and becomes more powdery, then move on to the next patch. Each patch may take a minute or two.

Patience and methodical work is the key here.

The result is what you've worked for – a finish that is durable, resistant to damage from knocks, resistant to water damage, able to 'breathe' through the unsealed backside, and it doesn't require waxing.

If you absolutely must wax the timber grain, at least wait for six weeks for all the solvents in the lacquer to finally escape. Otherwise, the residual solvents will interact with the wax and its solvents… the result may be crow's feet type crazing.

PART 4: INVOLVING OTHERS AND A FINAL WRAP-UP

Spare Parts and Trim - Hunting and Gathering

Before the age of agriculture, humans lived as hunter-gatherers. Men did most of the hunting, (though women could ensnare and kill small animals if needed) and women did most of the gathering. In doing a car restoration, you will most likely need replacement parts or assemblies. With this book concentrating on interiors, we will touch on how to utilise our hunter-gatherer instincts.

In my restorations, I have found much value in raiding wrecker's yards for replacement parts. The self-serve yards were best, as prices are cheaper and you can be open to serendipitous discoveries where you're not looking.

I could find seats and interior trim items that were in better condition than those same items already on the car. With some makes and models, it was possible to upgrade to a more luxurious interior, as explained previously in this book.

Is a gauge glass scratched or broken? Source another one. Has the gauge stopped working? Source another one. You may not know there and then whether it works either, but it's a better than even chance that it does.

Has the blinker indicator arm broken? Unbolt a whole assembly and replace it. Cracked centre console? Unbolt another one. When you get home, you can do a complete swap or interchange the best bits from each assembly into a superior example for your ride.

Snaffle those switches! Unroll those carpet underlays. Grab a better gearshift handle. Interior mirror corroding at the edges or unable to switch to anti-glare position? You know what to do.

Sometimes it's a bit harder to find exactly the parts you are looking for. Your make and model might be rare or already gone from the stock of most wreckers' yards. Here's where you need to think outside the box.

Are there similar models using the same switchgear or components? Think of GM's ubiquitous 'J-Cars' of the Eighties. Remember that joke about what's the difference between a Chevy Cavalier and a Cadillac Cimarron? I think the answer was 'about $500'. Or take Chrysler's front-wheel-drive brethren of that era. Do you think that each make and model used unique components?

It's more likely with smaller things but the principle holds true. The same parts can be found in Volkswagens as BMWs or Mercedes-Benzes. They just have different part numbers and different prices, if bought from a car dealer. Knowing what swaps with what is a valuable asset.

So bring your wife or girlfriend with you to the wrecker's yard. Ask her to dress in work jeans and shirt – it can be dusty work.

Bring some tools, plastic bags for small parts, a spraycan of WD40 or penetrating oil, drinking water, old newspapers and hand cleaner for removing some of the grime.

Importantly, bring a shopping list, because that's what you'll be doing – shopping for parts. But you may have to hunt them down before they can be gathered.

Here's where your lady comes in. The same neural network that retailers try to trigger as a shopping impulse is used in the hunting and gathering of spare parts. She'll grasp what you're looking for and help you find it. Clambering around and through wrecked cars won't even be a problem when she's hunting for that elusive part.

She can also hold up the hatchback or keep the door open so you can crawl in and start undoing bolts or unscrewing assemblies. It's a team effort and will be a bonding experience. Your lady might also come to understand what you wish to achieve in your restoration project and become more involved with it in general.

There'll be lots of broken glass about, which, being toughened, will fortunately not have sharp edges. Beware of any other sharp edges or corners, which may abound in a partially dismantled vehicle. Be each other's eyes when clambering or crawling in awkward positions.

Once you have your replacement bits, you can clean and polish them or paint them if necessary. Vacuum seats, carpets and soft furnishings well, particularly before they are installed. You'd be surprised by how much dust they can collect.

Found rust under your car's carpet? There's only so far you can go in restoring interiors before having to focus outwards towards the surrounding body and underlying mechanicals. And that means that you're ready to venture there using Volume 2 of this edition on *Low-Cost Car Restoration*.

Or maybe not. You might be now perfectly happy with the interior and the rest of the vehicle's fine. Fair enough. Go in peace.

But you'll want to see the bonus Appendices with useful stuff on maintenance and extreme maintenance. It may sound boring, but trust me, it's not when you're doing it. And you lengthen the useful life of your vehicle and save on repair bills down the track. You've already paid for it in this book, so go on, take a peek!

Vol. 2: Brilliant Bodies and Marvellous Mechanicals

PART 1. ORGANISE YOURSELF

One at a Time

Multi-tasking is great—or maybe not. If you have a number of restoration projects that you're aching to begin, PICK ONE! Even if you have a vast shed or working space, with adequate lighting and room, undertaking two restoration projects at the same time dilutes your efforts. Your progress appears slower. There's nothing more demoralising than to keep returning to restoration projects that just keep on and on, without any apparent end.

This leads to emotional and psychological burnout and an abandoned project, or possibly selling the whole thing. An unfinished project, with a body hulk vaguely resembling an automobile and many boxes of parts is a sure-fire way of losing money. It would be worth pennies on every dollar you spent on it. Finish your restoration project before starting the next one. It gives you the advantage of enjoying your result while working on the next project, and the broad spectrum of experience you've gained will make the next one easier.

Your Garage Shopping List

Scour your local rag's ad columns for garage sales. The alternative to paying full retail is to find some of these things at garage sale prices. Go online at various buy/sell sites which have an area-specific search-ability. Check out the freebie sites. E-bay is also useful for both new and second-hand items. Look for the following useful items:

* Large, heavy pot plant base with casters, for moving around heavy objects (but not too heavy)
* Plastic goggles
* Disposable paper breathing masks
* Extendable magnet on extendable aerial-type rod
* Work lamp, preferably one using a household light fitting and light bulb inside a cage. I prefer a filament bulb, as the colour spectrum matches the sun's and it doesn't flicker like a fluorescent device.

You can buy an inexpensive pair of plastic goggles from your hardware retailer. Wear them when working with a power tool like a grinding wheel or Dremel tool. Wear them when you're lying on your back under the car and peering upwards while scrubbing or brushing off dirt, or when applying a rust converter, paint or fish oil. There are lots of useful products but none of them belong in your eyes.

Nor does grit. There's nothing like grit in your eye to madden you, make you clench your teeth, groan like a wounded bear and blindly stumble away to the nearest faucet or open body of water.

Save your eyes.

And for that matter, save your back. These are both vital to your continued role as a functioning human being. Those with back problems or damaged eyesight will attest to how important. Don't allow an accident to rob you of vital personal resources.

Never lift heavy things if you can avoid it. If space is limited and there is no room to bend over to pick up something, it's probably not a good idea to do it anyway. Always use your knees to lift with and keep your back straight. If your space is so confined that you can't even reach down to do that, then this is one time when 'kicking the can down the road' type activity is actually recommended.

Raid your local garden nursery (or put this on your garage sale shopping list) for a pot plant stand on wheels. They are designed for heavy pot plants and have castors so that you can move them around without lifting. You can move some sub-assemblies around the garage with one of these but stop short of something like an engine block!

Try not to bend over when attending to tasks near the ground. If possible sit on a lower stool or on the ground itself. Or lie down. A plastic tarpaulin can be used to keep you off the ground, and you could use some outdoor furniture cushions for comfort if conditions are reasonably clean.

You can pack these cushions inside plastic shopping bags to guarantee protection from dirt.

Bag It and Tag It

When dealing with boxes of bits in the middle of a repair or restoration project, the likelihood of losing track of specific items is very high.

Label everything! Label everything with a marker. You can attach a tag of masking tape to a part or assembly and label that with a marker. Use a pen for cramming more information such as whether to repair the part or whether it's ready for use.

Paper bags for rust-prevention – fit steel or chromed parts into paper bags. The bags will 'breathe' and prevent the build-up of moisture, as might happen with a plastic bag. You can even lightly oil them with a household oil to prevent any corrosion, the way they used to do decades ago.

Plastic bags for non-rusting items – if it's plastic or rubber or other non-rusting parts, by all means bag them in plastic. Group them together if they go together, such as for a car interior.

Plastic bags for scuff prevention – use them as liners between heavy or delicate parts that are stored in open air in your garage. It will prevent surface damage and if bunched, the bags can act as cushions too. A sharp edge or point won't dent a neighbouring part if it is bolstered with a bunched-up plastic bag.

Polystyrene packing makes great footpads under stuff. It prevented your boxed TV from damage during delivery. Now those polystyrene packing blocks can keep large items off the garage floor. Things such as panels that you are leaning against the garage wall need to be kept off the concrete floor. In the event of a rain intrusion or spill, they won't get wet.

Take photos as you go. These become invaluable as instructions for later on. They use this approach in workshop manuals successfully, so you can too. A picture is worth a thousand words, particularly a good, digital colour picture. You can take them with digital cameras or even your mobile phone – whether it's 'smart' or dumb.

So take photos of an assembly in place, then at each stage of removal and disassembly. Show your other hand in the picture if you can, to point to significant places, like the bolt that has to be replaced first when re-assembling.

This can also show how rubber seals were installed by the factory. Knowing this can save you hassle later when your doors or bonnet or hood won't fit properly because the rubber seals were incorrectly replaced.

Download your pictures at the end of the day to your computer, and label them. Or at least number them in a sequence. Place the lot in a folder appropriately named. You don't want to recreate a time-wasting garage search on your computer!

Screws and Bolts Wire Together for Plating – if you intend to send screws and bolts off to the chrome plater, here's a way that prevents them from being lost in the chroming tanks.

First, arrange your bolts and screws in the order in which they will be returned to your car. Lay them out in a line, as they will be when used to re-attach a fender panel to the body inner panel, for example.

Next, take a length of galvanised wire, about 22-gauge, and wrap it around the threads of the bolts and screws. Several turns around the threads are fine to ensure that they don't fall off. Tag the wire assembly to identify it then send it to the plater's.

Though the plating will not cover all the screw and bolt threads, these surfaces will be hidden, indeed covered, when the fasteners are returned to their place in the vehicle. Moisture will generally not reach the threads and rust will not follow.

When returned from the platers, store the screws and bolts as is, still on the wire. The wires can be hung like string, taking very little storage space, less than if they were all in a jar or can. Once they are needed, they can simply be unwound from the wire and bolted into place.

Small boxes for parts – whether cardboard or paper, small boxes can be useful for storing clumps of small items such as particular screws or trim items, even a small assembly like a wiper motor. Label the box on the top and at least on one side. If you stack it with other boxes, you will want to see at a glance what the contents are without having to take down a box and open it up. Keep the parts in their boxes. Don't take them out until you need them – or to remind yourself what they are. If the boxes are labelled properly, you should know their contents.

Plastic meat trays for sorting and keeping small parts – these are open trays, so not useful for storage if you want to keep off dust. However, for temporary sorting during an active work, they are fine. If you have space on your work bench, you might even tape down a few with masking tape, so that they rest around the perimeter of the bench. If they're accidentally knocked, they won't spray their contents all over the place.

Plastic meat trays are also useful for cleaning small parts within them. Use an old toothbrush for this task but with soaps or detergents only, as solvents will attack the plastic tray. You can't be too anal about all this. Imagine losing half an hour of time looking for some part two months after you put it away. Now picture yourself going to a list or diagram and locating that part in one minute. Is it worth the extra time to record it's whereabouts originally? Of course it is! Bag it and tag it!

Bubble Wrap Saves Surfaces from Accidental Damage

You can use odd sheets of bubble-wrap to loosely wrap around objects or surfaces that may be damaged by sharp edges or bulky items you're struggling with installing or removing. If its reasonably clean when you're finished, roll the bubble wrap up and store it for another day. If you're feeling frustrated with the slow progress of your repair or restoration, you can even pop some of the bubbles!

For storing painted sheet metal or glass windows, tape cardboard sheets to one side of each piece, then stack the panels sandwich-wise. The glass and panels must be fairly flat to stack.

Putting It Back Together

When you're ready to re-assemble your parts into a restored sub-assembly, retrieve them from your bagged and tagged filing and parts storage system (remember?). Lay all the parts out before putting them together. It should look a little like an exploded diagram from your workshop manual. Have the parts all been cleaned, renewed and restored to your satisfaction? If not you'll immediately see what you've missed.

Car Covers

Car covers for cars kept outside are not a good idea. They'll trap moisture and promote rust on the body. Light dust covers for clean, dry cars kept in the garage are ok. If the car is dirty, then the act of pulling a cover over it may scratch the paint.

The best all-round protection for the car is a coat of wax and parking indoors. Next best is a coat of wax and parking under a car port type cover. The worst protection is being dirty, unwaxed and parked under a tree. Sap and leaf debris can fall and accumulate in odd corners of the bodywork and birds will drop their dubious blessings at random over it.

As a footnote, all bets are off when a hailstorm approaches. Park the car under a tree if there's no other cover and load on several layers of soft or heavy blankets. You can always wash and dry the blankets later, but hailstorm dents are difficult and very expensive to fix. Even empty and upside-down boxes of cardboard or polystyrene thrown onto the top panels of the car can make a handy barrier if nothing else is at hand. They may blow off, so use some bungee cords to tie them down to the roof gutters or to hook in the gaps between panels. Be careful of any metal to metal contact here.

For Discarded Gucci Knock-Off Bags

Use old travel bags or your girlfriend's discarded handbags to hold your polishing cloths and rags. Be tidy: hide the bags so your friends will never know! (I wrote 'Gucci Knock-Off' in the title. If it was the genuine thing and your girlfriend wants to get rid of it, sell it on E-Bay. You may get enough money to buy a lot of paints and materials for your restoration!)

PART 2. MECHANICALS & UNDERBODY

Degreasing Reveals the Awful Truth

To find out the truth about your engine bay or vehicle underside, degrease it. Once clean, things to repair such as flaking paint, corroded surfaces or cracked hoses will become apparent. Here's a step by step method of using inexpensive degreasers to find out what lies beneath.

Wear a pair of kitchen gloves while you degrease. Be aware that after you've used the following degreasers they won't be 'kitchen' gloves anymore! Store them in the garage thereafter.

Keep empty spray detergent bottles – especially the ones with a pistol grip and squeeze trigger. They're handy to have, as you can refill them with all kinds of liquid products like the degreasers mentioned here. Label their contents with a marker in case you forget what's inside.

The first degreaser is dieseline – apply from a spray bottle or brush it on. Try to keep it off your hands – it stinks and it's hard to wash that smell off. You can apply dieseline liberally as a degreaser: it's cheap and fairly effective on the really grimy stuff. Pour it into an empty spray bottle that had been used for a detergent or other household product. You can spray or stream it where you want it. You can also simply slosh it on as well. Use an old dish scrubbing brush, preferably one with a long handle, to work the dieseline into the grimy crevices and nooks.

THE AWFUL TRUTH?

Wrap electrical accessories such as the alternator with a plastic bag, and tie them with elastic bands. You want to be able to use the water spray freely without the hazard of drenching electrical devices. Lightly use a hose and water spray to remove the dieseline and dirt.

It's best to start with the dieseline, as it is itself an oil, and will leave an oily residue. Once you are finished with it, you can proceed to the secondary degreaser.

Take care if you spill diesel onto the ground – it will become as slippery as a mossy rock.

The second degreaser is kerosene – from a spray bottle or brush it on. This is a finer oil and closer to being a solvent for degreasing purposes. You will probably need to use less kerosene than the dieseline you've used.

Kerosene too leaves an oily residue but this is far less noticeable. You would only need to continue past the kerosene on selected areas or objects under the hood.

The third degreaser is a detergent. This is the final stage for those areas which are most obvious or receive the most attention, such as the air cleaner housing or an engine valve cover. Again, from spray bottles is best for covering a surface. You can dilute the detergent or spray it on neat.

A final, dainty degreaser is what you spray out of a can marked 'degreaser'!

On a side note, be very careful with alkaline degreasers. If they spatter in unexpected places, they will damage your paintwork before you know it. Avoid applying near painted surfaces. If you must use an alkaline degreaser, have a handy bucket or spray bottle of water. Learn from the author's mistakes!

Rust-Proofing Brackets

In your engine bay, there are a multitude of mounting brackets for engine sub-assemblies and accessories. They may be of cast or stamped metal or even plastic.

When you're mucking about with something, have a look at the related bracket. You now have temporary access to it. Clean it and see if it's rusty or corroded. Has the paint worn off?

Remove it if you can for easy degreasing, de-rusting and prepping and final painting. Or you may be able to do this with the bracket in place. Mask off or protect the surrounding areas, especially if you will be spraying something. Always have rags standing by to wipe with.

The method is covered in more detail below. Some parts will require painting with an engine enamel if they are attached to the block or near an exhaust manifold. Shiny plated parts, such as windscreen wiper motors with caps plated in nickel-cadmium can be covered by a clear lacquer or urethane to protect their lustre. Ensure you spray paint with a fine mist to prevent unsightly runs.

Some unpolished, unpainted metal brackets or parts can be brightened with a coat of silver paint.

This is a piece of 'Heightened Reality' as discussed in *Vol. 1: Impressive Interiors*, in this edition.

Masking Tape Stores Shavings

If you are drilling a small hole to install a factory extra or custom item and your car is basically already restored, you can save some bother in the cleaning up process afterwards.

You already know to apply masking tape to where you are going to drill, right? It gives the drill bit some 'grip' so that it won't wander away from the spot you want to drill through, and do surface damage.

So use some more masking tape and stick it onto the panel or bracket by an edge, so that the sticky part is facing upwards. When the metal shavings and flakes of paint are flung out by the action of the drill, they will be caught on the masking tape like flies to flypaper and be easily removable.

You don't know what flypaper is? Never mind.

Cuddling Your Coil

This is an improvement more than a restoration, although why not follow the leaders in automotive technology if you can? Neoprene boots around coils and distributors appeared first in Japanese luxury cars and spread from there. They are used to protect the coils from water splash or dirt from engine and road grime.

Buy some sheet neoprene about 1/8"thick. Remove your coil and wrap it

round with the sheet. Mark it to size including marking off the slot you will have to remove for the coil mounting bracket.

Once you have cut out the sheet and test-fitted it around your coil, you can approach your lady for a set of snap fasteners and install them at a convenient end of the neoprene sheet. Or you can simply use a plastic toothed cable tie – the disposable type. Use a black one to blend in. Either way, re-install the coil and connect it up. The negative terminal should connect to the distributor and the positive terminal to the ignition source.

If the coil is high and dry in the engine bay, you needn't take this extra step. Just wipe it clean and ensure all the connections are firm and clean.

If the coil is sitting pretty on top of your engine, you don't need this task either. Ignition coils have resistors that hold down the input voltage to the coil at about 9 volts during normal engine running. This is to prevent the coil from overheating. As it may be already hot when bolted to the top of your engine, wrapping it in a blanket may not be a good idea.

Hoses Saved by Sacrificial Sheet

Another thing to wrap protectively is any engine hose or rubber tube that is in danger of being cut or worn through.

Engine bays are busy places these days. Gone are the times when you would lift the hood and see everything laid out clearly, either attached to the engine or nestled out of the way on the firewall. Clearances between components have shrunk and shrunk again, as auto engineers have sought to cram more and more mechanical parts into smaller and smaller spaces.

This is partly due to efforts to make cars smaller so that they will be lighter and more fuel efficient. I believe that it also might be to make working in engine bays so difficult that the owner gives up and either hires mechanics or trades the car in on a new one. Conspiracy theory or fact? You decide.

Whatever the causes, the results are obvious. With some modern vehicles, you can't even stick your arm in anywhere without removing some sub-assembly first.

In this tight environment, coolant hoses and smaller air hoses could touch another surface and chafe against it from the movement of the engine or merely from vibration. The wear can be almost invisible until it ruptures.

So it is a good idea that after you have degreased your engine bay, you inspect your hoses to see whether they rub against anything or whether they have suffered some surface damage as a result.

Minor abrasions are not serious; cuts are a different matter. Small air hoses with a nick or cut can be repaired until you replace them. Just clean the short length around the cut with a wipe of detergent or thinners, then wrap the hose around the cut with PVC tape. For the minor vacuum pressures that these hoses operate on, this will be sufficient.

For larger hoses such as radiator coolant hoses, abrasions must be prevented from getting worse. Sometimes the hose was installed incorrectly. Untighten one end and without removing it, give it a twist so that it clears the obstruction. You may need to untighten and twist each end of the hose, one at a time. You can reduce the amount of coolant you lose during this operation by opening the coolant filler cap. This removes the internal pressure of the cooling system. Place the opened filler cap upside down, or somewhere obvious so that you don't forget to replace it later.

If the twist method does not clear the obstruction, you can wrap the hose in a sacrificial layer of sheet rubber. You can buy various thicknesses of rubber sheet and it's a good idea to have a small selection for different uses on hand.

I was faced with this problem on my Rover 3500 SE: the top radiator hose was resting on the air-conditioner compressor housing. The movement between the fixed radiator and a component bolted to a vibrating engine was starting to wear down the hose at this point. A minor twist would not move it away and there was nowhere else for the hose to go. It was an unfortunate combination of a US Federal specification engine bay coupled with the right-hand-drive arrangement of an Australian market car.

To solve this problem, I did the following modification:

Measure the length of the hose affected by abrasion with another surface, then add at least the same length again to each end. This gives you the total length of hose to wrap. Use this measurement as the length of the rubber sheet you are cutting off.

Next, take the rubber sheet and wrap it around the hose. Mark the circumference on the sheet with a crayon or chalk. This avoids the need for measurement and calculation. You now have the width of the piece of sheet you are cutting out. Add a small extra amount of width to create some overlap.

Now mark the piece you will be cutting out and place it on a cutting board (or expendable plank of wood on a table). Score and cut it with a Stanley knife or similar edge. A hacksaw blade will also do the job.

Wrap the coolant hose with the rubber sheet and move it about. When you are satisfied that you have the sheet around the right length of hose, take two plastic cable ties and use them to tighten the sheet around the hose. Ensure they are tight, without actually squeezing the hose. If the ties are in black plastic, they will be almost invisible, as will be the wrapped sheet rubber on the hose.

Cut off the excess ends of the cable ties with a pair of pliers. This makes the modification neater, and the ties will not become a nuisance if you have to work around them later, nor will they poke you in the eye.

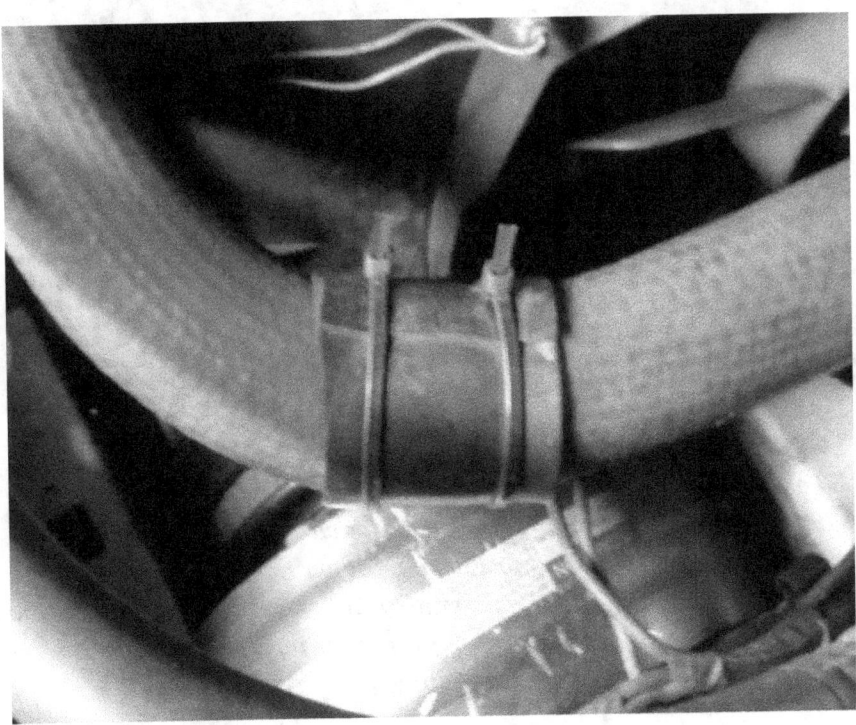

Radiator coolant hose wrapped protectively in rubber sheet to prevent abrasion on air-conditioner compressor beneath. Cable ties keep the sheet in place.

You can return later to your modification to see how it's getting on. If the sacrificial sheet rubber is wearing away, you can rotate it to a fresh spot. You can also move the wrap lengthwise along the hose. Eventually, after long periods of time and use have worn many parts of it, you can simply replace it with a new one.

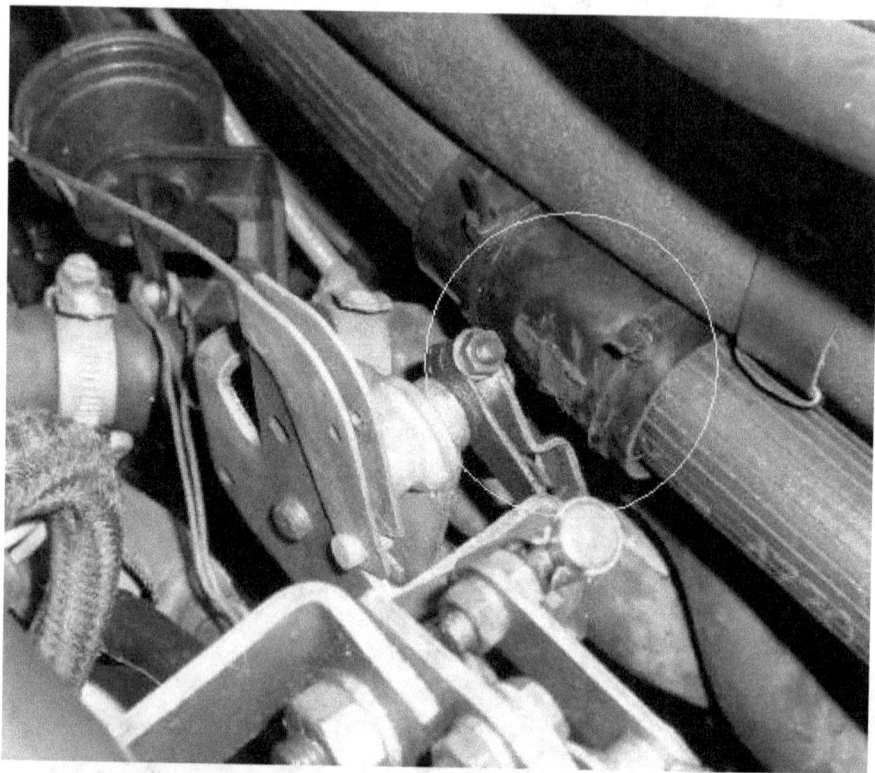

The air-conditioner hose has been wrapped with a sacrificial rubber sheet. Note the abrasion on the sheet (circled) caused by the throttle linkage nearby. If the air-con hose is punctured, then an expensive repair and re-gassing of the system follows. You can move the wrapped sheet around to even out the wear until a mechanic can re-adjust or replace the engine mountings.

For fuel line hoses, if they are perished, they must be replaced ASAP with matching fuel rated hoses. If the fuel hose is upstream from the fuel pump, it is particularly vulnerable as it is under pressure from within. (The same goes double for brake hoses. Replace them with new brake hoses as they are under even more pressure.) New fuel hoses have the added benefit of being formulated to withstand the presence of ethanol in the fuel. (More on the effects of ethanol in the Appendices section.)

You can wrap a hose with sacrificial sheet rubber while undertaking the painting and detailing of the engine bay as described below. It may be the very thing to do while waiting for some painted components to touch dry.

Paint Lifts with Oven Cleaner

If you have a part or suspension piece or body area that's difficult to strip paint from with a wire brush or liquid stripper, don't despair. Difficult contours or area access can be overcome with a can of simple oven cleaner.

Mask the area you want to treat if it's still in the vehicle. Spray the oven cleaner on and give it time to work. It will soak through old grease and paint and lift it off, right down to the bare steel. Rinse with water to remove the acid and the detritus.

Before You Paint the Engine

Once you have taken the steps described above to degrease your engine and engine bay, you will be ready to paint it. But not yet – there's one more step to go.

If you have a spray gun or even an air brush, then spray the engine with lacquer thinner. With the air brush it will take longer. Be careful to mask off everything else not needing paint, and be aware that thinners will attack plastics such as your goggles. It may be better to brush it on with a small brush, depending on the area you have to cover and the ease of access.

Gravity is your friend, so use it. Start at the top and work your way down to the bottom. This method will clear oil residue from a rough surface such as an iron casting. Lacquer thinners dry very quickly, so patience is unnecessary – as soon as you're done, prepare for the painting process with masking off tasks.

Paint your engine using the correct colour if you can. Proprietary colours for GM or Ford or Mopar engines are available in aerosol cans off the shelf, so it's easy to be authentic. Shake the can well before spraying, as you want to get as much pigment on as you can. Use only engine enamels – ordinary paint will flake off with the heat.

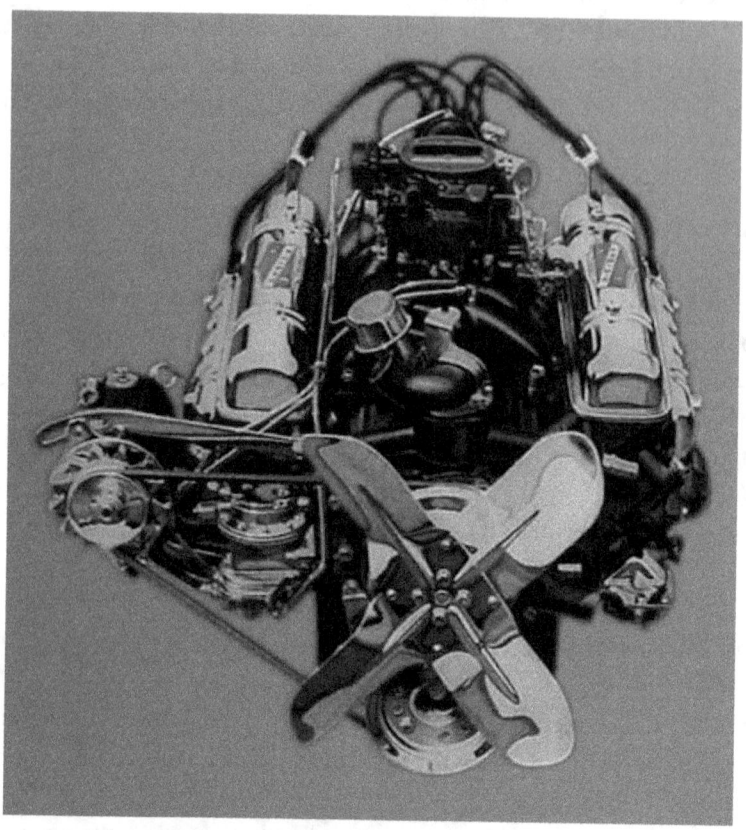

A finished engine is a thing of beauty – especially with as many chromed parts as this '55 Buick 'nailhead' V8. The black enamel presents no problems in colour-matching.

To get into tight corners, save the thin plastic tube that comes with a can of WD40, and insert it into your spray can nozzle. If it fits, use it! You can now spray paint in a localised spot in a difficult to reach area. Take all normal precautions against overspray. Remember to clean out the plastic tube with thinners or fine wire. It doesn't take much to clog such a narrow tube.

Another grade of heat-resistant paint is best for exhaust manifolds. These components are often even hotter than engine blocks and require specialised coatings. Find out whether you need a silver, black, white or iron-grey manifold colour to have a correct look. Of course, if you're going custom, then that's up to you. The same pant can be used on disc brake callipers or brake drums.

Black Power Under the Hood

If you are finishing off your engine compartment, take a can of gloss black lacquer and enough masking material, and work your way over all the black components in the engine bay. It will help if you've just done the final degreasing and you've idled the engine afterwards to evaporate any water and so that the surfaces are hot.

Start from the bottom and work your way up. This way, you will avoid leaning on any recently painted surfaces.

Use pages of shiny papered junk mail or rags and towels as masking aids. Drape them or tape them so that they protect bright components like carburettors or colour painted parts like the firewall or engine block. You can use small offcuts of cardboard as hand-held paint shields. A straight-edged sheet here and there prevents the black lacquer from straying. If a cardboard sheet become sticky or wet with paint along an edge, discard it for another one. Cardboard's cheap but your time and effort is valuable.

Have a rag handy that you can wet with lacquer thinner. If there's overspray on an unpainted component, you can moisten the rag in a small spot and use it to remove the overspray, working lightly. A cutting compound paste will work around sensitive areas which might be damaged by thinners, such as around decals or on previously painted surfaces.

Use the normal precautions: protect your eyes with goggles, have a disposable paper mask and a handy work light to show up all those little corners.

Remember the radiator – you can paint that black too if need be. Finally use the thinner-moistened rag and wipe all the hoses and wiring clean.

You can renew silver-painted parts with silver and some shiny alloy components could benefit too. But the next step in bringing your engine bay to showroom condition is clear.

A Clear Case for Gloss and Glamour

There's a lot of gloss and glamour that passes for news these days. Celebrities are by definition special and 'not like us', yet there's an enormous tabloid industry devoted to tearing them down again to show envious people that they're 'just like us' after all. Only richer. And considerably more famous.

I don't care one way or another what Celebrity 'A' had for breakfast or who's sleeping with Celebrity 'B's ex-husband's girlfriend's gym instructor.

But there is a way of making your engine bay look like a celebrity. It's just like other engine bays, but a lot more special. Interested?

Professional car detailers recommend using clear lacquer spray to lift a clean engine compartment to a higher level. Polished metal components like alloy intake manifolds, radiator caps or nickel-plated brackets and assemblies can be coated with gloss lacquer that will bring out the brightness of the alloy. Black hoses and even electrical wiring can also be given a sheen like they were just made. Done right, you can make it look as if your car just came from the factory.

Use the same precautions as you took spraying black lacquer, described above. Also work from bottom to top, and from the centre towards the outside of the engine bay.

Preventing overspray with appropriate masking, use short bursts of spraying. Move the aerosol can evenly while spraying to cover an area. Avoid thick, heavy coats. They will almost certainly run. Do several light coats.

Remove obstacles like hoses and wiring wherever possible. You can tie them back temporarily or just hold them away with your other hand. You can even use a short section of garden hose to mask a spark plug. Just remove the lead, place the hose on the plug and you have one less obstruction in that area.

Spray unpainted metal assemblies like headlamp housings, black plastic objects like air cleaners and clear plastic components like windscreen washer bottles and radiator overflow tanks. Spray clear lacquer on fan blades and around the radiator.

If the painted finish of the inside fenders and firewall is dull but free from chipping and scratches, it can be sprayed over with a clear, gloss coat. That way, you don't have to find or mix the original colour to get a just-resprayed look.

The last thing is the underside of the bonnet (or 'hood' for U.S. readers). It must have been thoroughly cleaned previously. Now if the paint colour is scratch-free, you can cover it with a fresh gloss coat that will impress. Avoid spraying over any insulation pad by shielding the edges as you go. Use scraps of cardboard or plastic sheet with straight edges. Take care not to overspray around the panel outside edges.

Before spraying the hood underside, be extra careful about covering the front fenders and entire engine bay with a drop cloth, tarpaulin or masking sheet. Wait until the engine bay lacquer is dry before covering the engine bay.

Once you've repainted your engine and exhaust manifolds with the correct high-temperature paint, this will complete your engine bay detailing to showroom quality. All you need to complete the showroom display is to raise the hood and stand a smiling store dummy (dressed in a suit) beside it. That's supposed to be the showroom salesman by the way. And no, it's not a comment on his or her intelligence.

Re-Energise Your Battery Tray

You may have the misfortune of owning a vehicle which has had a leaky battery sometime in its history. The acid had attacked the paintwork in and around the tray and dribbled downwards to attack the inner mudguard panel too.

Fortunately, you can solve this problem the way you solve the general rust problem, detailed elsewhere. Once you have removed all rust from the area and treated it with the appropriate primer, you can paint it to match the finish in your engine bay. It may be body colour or more likely it is a sort of satin black. Colour matching won't be a hassle if that's the case.

Once all is dry, take pity on your battery: give it a nice, soft bed to rest on. I kid you not – a rubber mat for batteries can isolate them from some shock and a lot of vibration. Vibration may help to weaken the integrity of the metal plates within the battery over time. Ensure the battery mat is slotted for drainage, in case of water in the engine bay or – horrors – battery acid.

A flat plastic tray underneath the slotted battery mat would collect any acid if you are returning what you suspect is a leaky battery into service. Monitor this tray for any deposits when you check your engine oil.

Battery Negative – First and Last

And always remember when disconnecting a battery to unbolt the negative terminal first. This gives no chance for dangerous sparks. If you are removing and returning the battery, the negative terminal comes first and last – disconnect it first. Reconnect it last.

Going to Ground

While we're on the subject of electrics, ensure that all your grounding cables are connected. The negative battery terminal is grounded by a cable to the engine block. A cable strap grounds the engine to the body via the firewall. The wiring harness too is grounded.

If you don't ground your engine to your vehicle's body, all sorts of weird electrical problems will emerge that will puzzle and confuse most who encounter them.

Repair Rusted Headlight Buckets

Most headlamp assemblies are in open and well-aired positions. They may get wet from weather but will dry efficiently. Sometimes, though moisture or an accident with rust remover (phosphoric acid) will damage the metal surface of the headlamp bucket, causing it to rust.

You can repair it *in situ* or you may have to remove it from the vehicle.

If removing, go easy on the screw threads. Most headlamp bezels and buckets are held by Phillips-head screws, and these may be rusted or corroded tight. Allow a penetrating oil to do its work, or a generous spray of WD40, and perform some other task for a little while. On your return, you should be able to undo everything smoothly.

Wire-brush the metal until the surface is shiny, then de-grease and prep as described for the general rust repair. Spray it with two coats of primer and then with the appropriate paint. A Plasti-Kote paint spray can gives an excellent finish.

Inspect the rubber grommet that covers the electrical wiring and plug as it meets the headlamp socket. If it is torn or brittle, replace it. Or better still, repair it using a tube of silicone gasket maker. It comes out black, so will match the grommet.

Now you may have a problem – your repaired headlamp bucket looks much better than the one on the other side! Don't fret – just clean the other one and repeat the process with the paint. Take care to properly mask off the electrical connections. Now you have a matching pair and they're both protected from corrosion and rust.

Getting Under

When working under your car or truck, always have it supported by approved jacks or stands. Deaths have occurred from a vehicle collapsing onto a person underneath.

Use your tyre jack to raise the car, then put a jack stand there. Repeat the process as you move around all the corners. Buy jack stands new or put them on your garage sale shopping list. A trolley jack works fine, but still use a jack stand as a safety backup.

Once your vehicle is lowered onto its jack stands, give the front end a shake, then do the same at the rear. This will ensure that the vehicle will settle properly onto the stands and that they are well placed under chassis rails or appropriate

parts of box sections.

Never use just a wheel jack (or a series of wheel jacks). These are made expressly for the purpose of raising a corner of your car for changing a wheel. They are not safety rated for more. Never crawl under a car supported only by a wheel jack. You simply can't skimp here.

You can't replace a jack stand with a pile of bricks either. The wheel jack holding up your car might give way. Since your makeshift brick pier will never be exactly the right height you need, your car will fall to the top brick and could shatter it, thus collapsing down to the next level of brick. It's too late for regrets when you are lying next to some useless brick rubble with your rib cage pinned beneath your car and you can't muster the breath to cry for help!

Undertaking the Undercoating

Inspect your wheel arches and vehicle underside.

Undercoating is there for a reason – you want that protection of your metal surfaces, the ones coming into contact with sand-blasts of road grit, mud and water. With age, undercoating may become brittle and flake off, or be hit with stones and crack off. Underneath is a slight layer of zinc primer and not much else to protect the metal. Rust will come very quickly.

Apply your undercoat by spraycan or by brush. Protect your eyes with goggles and your nose and mouth (if spraying) by an inexpensive paper mask. Sometimes, so close to the ground, a gust of breeze can deliver dust or grit into your eyes. Come prepared!

As you do the wheel arches, move on to all the areas under your car.

If you don't have a garage creeper (something else for the garage sale shopping list), use a large sheet of cardboard, preferably of the size that carried a large domestic appliance. Depending on the surface underneath, you can slide on the cardboard, or the cardboard can slide with you.

Keep a large sheet or sheets of cardboard under your car or truck if it leaks oils and fluids from various places. (Don't slide on these though!) Old carpet can be used to soak up sump oil dripping from your vehicle. You can renew it as you see fit. Just remember that it may hold more dust than you may want blowing around the garage.

Inspect for oil stains on the underside. These will be like a plume, emanating from up forward, where the leak occurs. Usual sources are rear main engine seals, front engine (timing case) seals, auto transmission underpan seal, or even a steering box oil seal. The rear axle housing / differential may leak too, sometimes from the pinion seal, sometimes from the rear cover seal.

Some older cars and trucks have a natural aspiration hole on a solid rear axle, where a small trickle or moist, oily trail may be seen beneath the hole. These are normal and not a sign of bad sealing. One garage mechanic I once spoke to opined that I would need a new seal when he saw an oily trail beneath a deliberately drilled, tiny hole in the axle housing. Needless to say I never went there for mechanical repairs!

Wherever you see broken, flaked off or chipped undersealing, this needs to be rectified. Dealing with a spot of rust now is better than dealing with a spreading patch sometime in the future. Take a white crayon with you and circle the spots you find for later attention.

If you don't have a garage work light, deploy all the desk lamps that you can to cast light under the vehicle. You'll be surprised at how much you see.

Clean and degrease what you can. Use an old kitchen scrubbing brush with nylon bristles to dry-scrub dirt off. Dry brushing of dirt, grit and dry mud leaves less material to soak and carry moisture under your vehicle.

It also shows whatever is underneath that needs attention. I assume that you want to know the Awful Truth, or you wouldn't be down there.

Fix that Undercoating

Attend to these bare metal spots all at once. If you have the time (or the patience) apply rust converter (phosphoric acid) to the bare metal with the surface rust. Do this with a cheap, small brush. The acid attacks the bristles anyway, so you don't want a fine sable brush for this work. Sable brushes are for expressing yourself on a canvas, or for tickling your lover's –

Ahem. Never mind.

Once dry, wipe the excess rust converter with a clean rag then apply some spray primer. Once this is dry, spray on some undercoat. You can buy cans of this black, bituminous undercoat for a few bucks.

If your time (or patience) is limited, then use another inexpensive brush and a can of fish oil, and apply the fish oil to the crack in the undercoat.

You can be liberal here, allow the fish oil to fill all the crevices of the gap, and go past the edges. You want the metal to be sealed from further corrosion. It doesn't matter so much if there still is surface rust. It is trapped in the fish oil, and will not rust further. (That is, unless it is rusting through the panel *from the inside*. If this is the case, then that's a whole new ball game.)

Once the fish oil is dry, wipe it with a clean rag. Most oils are paintable once dry, though some oils stay sticky. Spray on your undercoat now, making sure to cover the spot and around it.

Always turn the can upside down and spray clean when finished. If you want to use all the undercoat or paint that you've paid for in that spray can, ensure that you keep cleaning the spray head.

Better yet, remove the spray can's little plastic spray head and soak it in some of the solvent used in the paint. You can use a spare spray can lid to soak it in, unless it has a little air hole in the bottom. Enamels use mineral turpentine, lacquers use thinners. You can use a little brush to help clean out the air passages.

If you need to remove undercoating, such as for a chassis or box section repair, use some oven cleaner in an aerosol can and spray it on. Let it sit for a couple of hours out of direct sunlight then use steam cleaning or high-pressure water blasts to remove the undercoat. Dry wipe it down and you now have access to the metal underneath for welding or whatever.

While You're There

OK, you've crawled under your car and truck. You've raised it securely so it won't drop on you and make you a good deal thinner (in a bad way, I mean). You may be cold, or hot. A breeze blows dust into your eyes and you remember to draw your clear goggles over them. You're almost certainly uncomfortable. So are you going to make the most of your position?

Hell, yes! So while you're attending to the undercoating, take some spanners or wrenches with you. With your fingers, try all the nuts and bolts you see. If you can turn them with your fingertips, I think you'll agree they need tightening.

You're not a prude, but you know that nudity has its place. So are there any bolt threads that are suspiciously naked? Should they be clothed (or accessorised) with a split washer and a nice, thick nut? Things have been known to fall off cars, and you don't want to lose a big bit that you need.

Like an exhaust muffler. Or a Panhard rod.

Replace any missing nuts you find. Search through your tins of nuts and bolts. Try several threads to find a match. Take several samples of nuts with you before you go back under. It's a hassle to go needlessly back and forth.

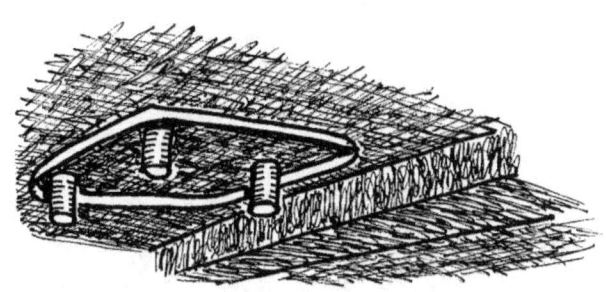

Naked bolt threads... no nuts in sight. Is something about to fall off?

A trip to the wrecker's should include a sampling of bolts and nuts from the kind of car or truck that you have. Get at least a handful, and preferably from different areas, such as the engine bay and underneath the vehicle.

Use a split washer wherever possible. If you have none, you can mount two nuts onto the same bolt thread. Almost completely tighten the first, then spin the other up the thread so that they are side by side. Then tighten the nuts simultaneously against each other, wrenching in opposite directions. They will compress against each other and against the thread itself, and this will work like a spilt washer. Take care not to overdo this and damage the thread.

Make a note of painted components or sub-assemblies under the vehicle, where the paint has been scraped or chipped off. Degrease and clean these areas. After the detergent, wipe over with a clean rag dipped in methylated spirits.

Colour-match it with similar paint. You can spray or you can brush – the finish will not matter so much underneath. Generally, under-body components are a sort of satin black. Try to avoid using a gloss black unless the clean surface was painted that way. It will look odd and stand out as a hurried repair. However, if it's plainly utilitarian and you don't care, then knock yourself out.

PART 3. BODY WORKS

Doing Battle with the Rust Demon

The Rust Demon (for so I have imaginatively named it) is a sly and cunning devil indeed. It works quietly and many times in unseen places.

You do not hear it nibbling like you may with termites in your house. Yet it does leave some telltale marks, such as tiny deposits of brown dust on the garage floor, or bubbles underneath the paintwork. At least the Rust Demon can be halted in its tracks and with inexpensive materials. But you will need to apply some serious elbow grease.

Look for rust where two or more body panels meet in a seam. Look where water may collect and stay. Inside the doors, where the outer skin meets the inner panel. Inside the floor of the boot, or 'trunk'; inside the fenders; behind rocker panels; underneath the carpeting on the floorpan; around the windscreen and rear glass trim; under the battery tray and even behind chrome trim strips or mouldings.

If it's serious, loose scale type rust, you can start scraping it off with a paint scraper or gasket scraper. A wire brush is next in line for rust removal.

Put on a pair of kitchen gloves and use some discarded steel wool. The wool can get into nooks and crannies that a larger wire brush cannot and the gloves can save some of your skin from the abrasion of using it.

A round wire brush can also be chucked into an electric drill or for small areas, you can do the same with a Dremel tool. Observe all the precautions here regarding your power cord and protecting your eyes with goggles and your breathing with a paper mask. Also, you may want to cover areas or parts of the vehicle with a tarpaulin to prevent dust and scale from being flung into hard-to-clean areas.

A really pitted or badly rusted panel can be treated with muriatic acid (from hardware stores) and a wire brush. Apply the acid and scrub vigorously with the metal brush. Do about a square foot of area at a time and allow a quarter of an hour. Wipe down and repeat if necessary. Then follow up with the usual rust converter - phosphoric acid.

When the underlying metal shows through as bare and shiny, wipe it down with a rag and a degreaser such as trichloroethane, or regular degreaser and methylated spirits. You want both a rust-free surface and a clean one.

The next step is to apply some red-metal-type primer that bonds properly with the metal. A variety of such are found in auto supply stores. Ask an attendant about the best primer for bare metal, not just for applying a coat of paint over it.

Use two coats of bare metal primer, allowing enough time for the first coat to dry. Be thorough about covering the area. No naked or rusted metal should show.

Ensure that the painted and intact areas around the one you're treating are also clean and degreased. There's no need to cover them with the primer, but you want all hidden painted areas to be ready to take your rustproofing.

Rustproofing material (such as Fisholeum, Waxoyl or similar) comes in spraycans or tins. Each has an advantage, and depending on the areas you are undertaking to treat, you may wish to buy both. The spray-on aerosols usually come with a thin extension hose with a multi-direction nozzle. This lets you get into otherwise inaccessible areas such as doors or other cavities and to apply the product within. Try for an even coverage and start at the top or as near to it as you can. The stuff will run down the surfaces within.

If there are drain holes, ensure that they are clear by cleaning them out with wooden ice cream sticks (clean ones, without sticky ice cream on them!). Place a small, clean container below these drain holes so that you can catch any excess that drips out. You can apply this excess to any accessible areas by brush. Why waste it and make a mess?

Some experts advise the practise of drilling access holes for your spray nozzle so as to gain sufficient coverage within. I'm reluctant to support this method, as it creates one more problem, that of a raw metal edge to that hole, and the need to find and buy a rubber plug for it.

Usually, there are already access holes awaiting your pleasure (pardon the pun) that the manufacturer put there. All you need to access them is to remove the rubber or plastic plugs sealing them, and to do it in a non-destructive way. In the majority of cases, I believe that using these methods of access (together with removing a door internal trim panel completely, which I also recommend) will give you enough access to clean, prep and treat interior surfaces that need it.

The rust-proofing product you're applying is designed to never harden completely, but to stay moist and water-proof the surface. In most cases, a simple fish oil is not the best product to use as it tends to remain sticky and attracts dust to itself.

Removing Rust from Trunks or Boots

See the advice given above for de-rusting, preparing and rust-proofing.

Once the rust has been scraped out, apply liberal amounts of red-metal-type primer and let it fill all cracks and seams. Now you should not apply a rust-proofing that remains moist (and perhaps sticky) because, after all, you want a clean boot area for carrying cargo, or other practical uses such as sneaking your teenage friends into the drive-in without paying. Just kidding —who does this any more?

You can either apply your final coat colour within the trunk area, or an impact-resisting paint that contains a measure of bitumen. It will give a wrinkled or uneven surface, which can be sprayed over when dry with a colour paint. If you don't mind the appearance or it's similar to the utilitarian paint finish that the vehicle came with, that's fine. This coating will prevent a lot of paint-scratching events from occurring in the future.

Whichever way you go, spray-painting colour within the boot or trunk needs only the use of an aerosol can. You don't need to use a spray gun, unless you are going for a show-winning finish. No colour-matching is needed, since the area is visually isolated from the outside body anyway. You can use lacquer or enamel equally well. Some people recommend a Plasti-Kote enamel spraycan as a higher quality product.

Once it's all dry, replace your trunk lining mats, etc. but not before cleaning and dressing them. If the jack is visible when installed, wipe it clean and lightly grease the working parts. Clean the spare wheel and tyre, dressing as desired. And pump up the spare! Consider the possibility of storing some small spare parts or car care products within the hollow of the spare wheel. Ensure they won't rattle.

If you are repairing a luxury car with a carpeted trunk, so much the better. Replace the lining pieces, ensuring that all attachments, bolts and screws are present.

When You've Found a Rust Hole

So what if you've cleared the Rust Demon away and found a hole? Let's say it's an inside panel or worse still, an outside one? Is it reasonably small (no bigger than you can put a hand through) and it's not in a structural place, such as a box section? Is it a flat or nearly flat panel?

If you've answered 'yes' to these questions, then that's still a repair you can do yourself, before buying a patch panel and / or turning it over to someone else.

If you happen to have some galvanised steel sheet of about the same thickness, that's best. If you have some scrap metal off-cuts of automotive steel sheet, that's fine too.

Using a pair of tin snips, cut away the jagged outlines of the rust hole, so you have a smoother outline.

Now take a sturdy G-clamp, and lightly tape a small ball bearing into the cup on the end of the screw-threaded bolt. The ball bearing has to be large enough to extend beyond the cup, so forming a rounded head. It is this rounded protrusion that will be needed.

Now insert the G-clamp so that the fixed side of the clamp is within the body or door cavity and on the other side of the panel. Align it so that it is next to the rust hole edge, but about 1" or 25mm from it. Turn the handle on the bolt so that you are clamping this spot in the metal panel. Tighten the clamp until you have made a dimple in the sheet metal.

Now undo the clamp and repeat the process around the perimeter of the hole. Use spacings of 2" (50mm) between dimples. If the hole is right on the edge of a panel, such as a door and you have no perimeter for the dimples, don't sweat. Take it as far around as you can. If you can surround the patch panel for about three quarters of its circumference, that should be enough.

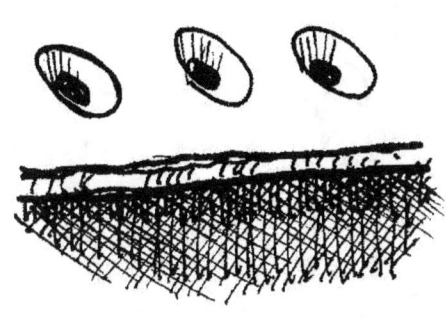

Centre punch each dimpled hole and use that to drill a 3/32" (2.38mm) hole into the metal. You want the holes to be in the dead centre of the dimples. Why? Because you'll be inserting sheet metal screws here and you want them to go in with their tapered heads flush against the rest of the metal panel.

Take your piece of scrap sheet metal and use tin snips to cut it to the same approximate shape as the rust hole. I say approximate, as it will have to be bigger than the hole, so as to take up all those screws you will be inserting in later. You should allow plenty of overlap, at least an inch beyond the screw holes, and perhaps two inches.

Wrap the patch panel with masking tape. Make a handle you can hold out of some of the tape. Insert the panel into the hole and adjust it with the tape handle so it is gently pulled flush with the inside of the panel.

Using a felt tip pen or small marker, mark through the holes you have made onto the masking taped surface of the patch panel. Don't move the panel once you're doing this. If you have an itch – don't scratch it. Now's not the time.

Once you've marked all the holes, remove the patch panel and drill holes of the same size through the marked spots. The tape will help to hold the drill bit, but use care and a low drill speed here, lest the drill bit wander away.

After all, drill bits have such short attention spans!

"DRILL BIT WANDERING AWAY..."

Once the holes are drilled, remove all the masking tape except for the handle on the front of the patch panel. You'll need this to manoeuvre it into place.

Now is also the time to wash and degrease the patch panel on the back (inside). Coat it with primer and a rust-proof compound as detailed above. Do the same with the inside of the body panel which has the rust hole. It's good insurance against rust starting within the seams of these two panels once they're in place. Watch out that you don't cut yourself on any sharp edges around your drilled holes on the inside panel!

Next, when all is dry, insert the patch panel into the body and screw in the first sheet metal screw. It should be a flat-topped or pan-headed type, preferable a non-Phillips head so you can tighten it more.

Once the first screw is in place and grabbing both sheets of metal, don't

tighten it all the way. Make sure it's firm then move on to the next screw. Once you have screwed them all in, tighten them. As you tighten the screws, it pulls the patch panel in towards the body panel. When you're done, use a rule or other straight-edge and place it over and around the repair, making sure that no screw head is proud of the panel surface. They should have all gone within the dimpled area.

Now apply body filler to the patched area and screws and sand it smooth, flush with the rest of the panel. Check your work frequently and follow the subtle curvature of the panel if it has one. The filler should be no deeper than the thickness of the body panel itself. Sand it with a 36-grit wet n' dry paper, finishing with an 80-grit paper.

Apply primer and sand it smooth. For primers, start sanding with 120-grit, followed by 180-grit and re-apply another coat of primer if necessary. Finish with 400-grit before painting. Use block sanding techniques. If the surface is fairly curved, use a sponge-like sanding block. If it's fundamentally flat, use a hard rubber block.

Sanding blocks are cheap and easy to buy, but if you want to avoid an extra trip to town or across suburbs, you can use an offcut from a wooden two-by-four. Make sure the offcut is straight and clean, then wrap your sandpaper around it and go block sanding.

Paint the panel, using advice found elsewhere in this book.

Where colour matching is not a problem you can use aerosol cans, but where it's exposed and visible, an aerosol may be OK but may not be colour-matched to the rest of the panel. If you can, use a small tin of body paint that you may have from an earlier occasion and apply it with a spray gun (or an air brush if you have one but only if it's a small area).

Otherwise a pro can be hired to do the job with professional equipment and facilities. It won't be that expensive, as you've done the hard preparation work already.

Resprayed areas are less visible if 'feathered off' at a natural join, crease or moulding. Ask the spray painter for the best spray paint coverage strategy here. Discuss also how many coats you want to have applied and the quality you want and cost you are willing to pay.

(You can finish off the paint job to an even higher standard by using the tips set out below, in the post-painting sections.)

A body filler repair isn't the best option around, as over the long term, if the filler is too thick and the filled area too big, stress cracks may appear as the metal expands and contracts differently to the filler. How thick? How big? There are estimates but nobody really knows. But we do know that for small, non-critical areas, it's the most convenient solution.

Take a Bath

You can drown the Rust Demon to oblivion by making your own acid dipping tank. For smaller parts and panels that are removable from your vehicle, a simple way of de-rusting them is to immerse them and let time and acid do the work for you.

Take some swimming pool acid, a sheet of plywood and thick plastic sheet (about 4mm). You can buy these from a hardware store. Make a frame from 2 x 4 timber along the outside edges of the plywood. Lay the heavy plastic sheet over this frame and staple it to the outside of the frame. You now have your acid dipping tank.

Mix your acid in a ratio of 1:2 hydrochloric acid to water. Pour the acid into the water, never the water into the acid. Protect yourself with gloves and goggles. Pour the acid mix into the dipping tank and you're ready to go.

Immerse parts for 30 – 60 minutes. Panels need to be generally flat for adequate coverage. For items that are too big to be completely submerged, turn them over after one area has been done.

If out in the open, keep infants and ducks out of this 'pond'!

When you see no more rust on the surfaces of the item, rinse it with water and dry it off with a clean rag. Coat it with a phosphoric acid rust converter, let that work awhile, then wipe off the excess and spray on the primer.

You can clean up when you're finished with some baking soda or bicarbonate of soda. Pour in two pounds (half a kilogram) of soda for every 10 U.S. gallons (8 Imperial gallons or 36.3 litres) of acid mix into the bath. This neutralizes the acid for disposal.

Once dry, you can stand the frame on its side and store your acid bath against a wall using the minimum of floor space.

Paintless Process for Panel Pounding

You don't have to join your local Lodge to make good use of a masonry trowel!

If you come upon one of those unfortunate little dents caused by the impact of a pointy thing, you will know the terrors of indecision. Do you go to the trouble of panel beating and spray painting a whole panel or do you try to ignore that little bugger of a dent? It's somehow worse if the paint is still intact within the little dent.

A pointy dent can also be convex. That is, it sticks out. This may have happened to a trunk lid or bootlid that was closed over a sharp, angular, bulky object.

Either way, if the dent can be reached from the convex side, this repair method can be tried.

The professionals would use a body hammer with a flat head and an instrument called a slapping spoon. Now, a slapping spoon is not one of those instruments of interest kept in a drawer under the marital bed. It looks like a masonry trowel, with a raised handle and a flat, rectangular blade.

The professional body man places the slapping spoon against the raised side of the dent and uses the flat-headed hammer to tap it in. With some care and common tools, you can do the same thing.

Select a trowel and remove any old mortar or grit, so that the blade is flat and clean. Wrap the trowel blade with masking tape so that there is no exposed metal. The professionals do this too, and it is so that the metal surface does not scratch the paint of the car's panel.

Select a hammer with an ordinary flat head. Choose a smaller one if you have one, in case you need to insert it within the vehicle cavity.

If the dent is convex (sticks up on the outside), you have more control over ambient lighting and how far you can swing your arm. Install a spotlight nearly parallel with the panel surface to throw a highlight onto the dent. If the dent is concave, use the same lighting technique, which would show the smallest dent as a shadow.

Use the hammer to tap the blade of the trowel. Take care to keep the hammer's flat head flat to the trowel. If you make a dent in the trowel by hitting it with the edge of your hammer head, chances are you'll also make a new dent in your vehicle. That isn't your intention!

Check your work frequently. Use a number of light taps then remove the trowel and examine the surface. Depending on the thickness of the panel, your progress will be fast or slow. Take your time here.

The same goes for those concave dents. Remove enough of the interior to gain access to the inside of the panel. You will need enough for your arms and tools. It will be difficult to actually see the inside of the dent because of the components in the way. If it is a door, there will be locking mechanisms and window lifting scissor assemblies and side intrusion bars and whatnot. You will likely have to go by feel.

Here it would be good to have a friend on the other side who can give you a commentary on your progress, so that you don't have to climb out and back in many times to check your progress. Your friend may be able to hold up a mirror and angle it so that you can see your progress while still inside, in your no doubt uncomfortable position. Your helper could also video record the dent using the macro lens on an iPhone and hand the device to you!

When the dent was made, it stretched the metal ever so slightly. This makes it harder to return the panel to a completely flat condition, but not impossible. You can reduce the depth of the pointy dent by about 80% to 90% using this method. Further progress must be more careful still to avoid raising a ring around the remnant of the dent.

The auto body professionals can overcome the stretched metal problem by cold-shrinking a dent out. To do this, they use a serrated dolly and a slapping file (I know, I know, it all sounds like it belongs in a private dungeon). The dolly is a metal form with a raised cross-hatch texture. It is held so that the textured surface is behind the dent and the slapping file is slapped against the panel on the opposite side. The metal panel is 'shrunk' or tightened up around the multitude of raised points on the dolly.

Forget using a meat tenderiser instead, as the texture is much too coarse!

There's a high likelihood of paint damage too. This method is best left to a panel which is being resprayed anyway, and by using the correct tools.

Once you have tapped your way to almost perfection, you can 'fill in' the remaining dentlet with a touch-up paint. You can use more paint if the colour is a non-metallic, since colour-matching is less difficult. Apply with an artist's brush and let it dry before adding a second layer if need be. To prevent paint runs, take care not to put too much on. Follow the hints on attending to stone-chips elsewhere in this book.

Picnic Cutlery Protects Trim

Somehow, you can end up with a lot of unused plastic forks, spoons and knives. They often come with a take-away meal and aren't used if you go home to your proper cutlery. Don't just leave those plastic implements in a drawer or throw them away. Bunch them together with an elastic band and store them among your garage tools.

The handles of this plastic cutlery can make good wedges or separators. The plastic knives are especially good for prising apart small parts that might become damaged if you use a screwdriver blade, or even an old metal knife blade. Use plastic knives as a lever to lift trim or mouldings off a panel without damaging the paint or trim. Use them to prise off an interior door trim from the metal inner panel.

If you have a multi-pin electrical plug and socket that you have to prise apart, a screwdriver would create sparking by earthing a live current. You can avoid having to disconnect your battery, especially if you're stranded somewhere and short on tools, if you use a plastic knife as a lever. It's non-conductive and using two knives on opposite sides means you can prise off both sides simultaneously.

Happy Bolts Have Clean Threads

Incidentally, keep all your bolt threads clean. A dirty or gritty thread can make it hard to tighten the nut, or even make it jump the thread entirely. Threaded bolt holes can be cleaned out with a thread tap. For exposed bolts, clean the bolt thread with a wire brush or steel wool if it's really dirty, then finish off with a rag and a penetrating oil like WD40. Paint overspray could be wiped off with solvent and a rag.

If the bolt is welded to a panel and there's slight damage to the thread, you can use a nut to re-align the thread. Use lots of oil or WD40 and a socket wrench to coax the thread back into shape. Tap the wrench handle with the heel of your hand. Reverse a bit then return to the resisting part. Use lots of care and patience here. The object is not to force the nut over the thread with brute strength, but to coax it along. Using the leverage of your socket wrench or ring spanner could easily twist the bolt off or shear it if you're not careful.

The edge of a thin metal file could be used to continue a trough in the thread though following the curvature of the bolt itself might be tricky.

These tricks will not overcome a severely damaged bolt, which if attached to a panel, must be removed and replaced by other means.

Bright Idea for Bright Bolts

If a bolt has been newly re-plated, you can prevent damaging the head when you tighten it in place. Wrap a strip of masking tape over the inside of your spanner or wrench. That way, you have no metal-to-metal contact and the delicate chrome or nickel plating will be preserved.

Before You Spray

If you have a bare metal panel to paint, you will have prepared it with a rust converter. These are usually based on phosphoric acid, so wear some kitchen gloves to save your hands from some uncomfortable burning.

Spray and wipe it over all of the bare metal to treat any tiny rust traces that may be left. It will also prevent any new rust from forming, but this is a very, very temporary state of affairs. Once you have waited the required time for the acid to do its work, wipe it off then follow up with this next step.

Take an old towel or clean rag and some lacquer thinner and wipe the panel with it. You will find black marks on the rag, so turn it to a new section of rag and continue wiping down. When you are finding no more black residue, you are ready to spray your primer coat. This extra step will ensure better adhesion of the paint.

Wear rubber or plastic gloves while handling the cleaned surface, so as to prevent the oils from your skin from affecting the surface adhesion.

(If for any reason you have some bare metal which you are unable to get to before it begins rusting (12 – 24 hours), cover it with masking tape. This prevents oxidisation until you are ready to apply rust converter and preparations for the primer.)

A significant proportion of body panels sourced from the factory have a problem. That black primer might have been sprayed at the factory over contaminated metal surfaces. It is best to treat new panels like old ones and strip and prep them down to bare metal before painting.

Spraycan Painting

For any spray painting done with an aerosol, warm the spray can in hot water first. The droplets will be finer as you spray. The can cools down as a result of the paint and propellant inside expanding and leaving the can. Keep it warm by returning it to your pot of hot water. If you're in a warmer climate, you won't need to do this.

Thin that Urethane

If your car was originally painted with acrylic lacquer, you can use the same type of paint. Or you can choose a modern urethane paint for its toughness and extra durability. The trouble is that if you thin it according to instructions, the result will tend to look thick and enamel-like. There will be more orange-peel to remove.

So thin your single-stage urethane paint (avoid the complications of a dual-stage urethane) twice as much as the instructions on the can. You will apply more coats but they will be thinner and the final result will be more impressive.

Easy Pourer for Precious Paint

Some paints are more expensive than others but basically all liquid colour is worth its weight in liquid gold when you throw in the cost of the labour to apply it and the facilities to apply it in.

Since you're doing much of the work yourself, the labour expense is not relevant here, but the cost of the paint is. Assuming you have a good spray gun and some reasonable facilities at home, you are in the market for pots of automotive paint.

You can reduce the waste when pouring out of the can by purchasing a paint tin pourer that snaps onto your can's rim. They come in several sizes for different tin diameters. They look like an open spout and can be bought from paint stores. Or you can make one yourself from masking tape.

Simply cut two lengths of about 8" – 10" (200mm - 250mm) of masking tape and fix them to the rim of the can. Overlap the two pieces halfway around the tin to make a stronger spout. Use 2" (50mm) wide strips of masking tape. If you have a narrower tape handy, you can double up with that in a length overlap.

Masking Materials for Spray Painting

Auto body shops use special plastic sheets to mask the car or truck they will be painting. This is not necessary for the amateur. Other materials can be used to protect the glass on windows or different panels or wheels from troublesome overspray.

House painters buy cheap, plastic drop cloths to place on floors to prevent paint spill from walls or ceilings. Painting a house wall with a roller can produce a veritable mist of paint and could speckle any surface not covered with a drop sheet. These plastic drop sheets are usually clear and come in rolls. Buy some and cut it into smaller rectangles, so that you have adequately large sheets for your auto work. If you don't want to cut a sheet up, they are also light enough to be folded over and taped up that way.

Do you need to do a spray job right now and can't go to the local hardware store? Go to your kitchen for your masking needs. Whenever you've bought something, chances are that you carry it home in a plastic bag. Rather than discard them, keep these bags as handy rubbish bags to line kitchen bins or whatever.

But more to the point, save all those plastic shopping bags and use them to mask off parts of your car when preparing to spray paint. Tape them up together as needed, being careful not to leave any gaps. Use masking tape here, as it doesn't matter. The bags will easily withstand acrylic (water-based) paints. The solvents in lacquers or enamels will attack them, so ensure that you are not too heavy with your painting. You'd want to get a good finish anyway, so you're less likely to be heavy-handed here. The double layers of a bag can be applied as is for masking. It will be sufficient to protect the underlying surface and to withstand the attack of solvents.

If the bags have been used more than once and become grimed with paint, replace them with fresh ones. Some of the paint may flake off the plastic sheet and possibly drift into the path of your spray can or spray gun. Replace them. There's no shortage, and shopkeepers give them to you with your shopping!

Plastic bags can mask such things as wheels and tyres. Door handles or other protrusions can be 'bagged' or wrapped over, to also protect them from overspray.

Do not under any circumstances use newspaper for masking! Newspaper pulp is poor paper, high in loose fibres and dust. Unless you're spray painting a matt finish which dries INSTANTLY, do not use newspaper. The air from your spray paint or even a light breeze will carry those paper fibres right onto your newly painted, wet surface. There they will stay, unless you ruin your finish with a fingertip to remove them, or polish them out much later when dry (and be ready to apply that layer of paint again).

You wouldn't hire a moulting dog to do your spray painting for you, would you? Enough said.

The best paper to use for masking comes to you free!

Be sure to remove that 'No Junk Mail' sign from your mailbox, and every week (almost every day) some helpful person will be giving you masking paper for your project.

Why junk mail? It's printed in bright colours to entice you to buy those supermarket specials or clothes or garden sheds. This requires a gloss paper for best results. Glossy paper will not shed fibres like newsprint. Granted, the pages are smaller, but you can easily masking-tape them together for all the coverage you need. And they are usually stapled together for your convenience. Just be careful how you remove the staple so that it doesn't leave a hole for paint to find a way through.

Tapes for Masking

Professionals use specialised tapes to mask their work ready for spray painting. You can do the same, but if you don't happen to have it, or your budget is tight, try the following.

Use masking tape to attach your masking sheet to the panels. Make sure it's pressed firmly to the surface, as sprayed paint can work up under the edge of masking tape if it isn't firmly pressed to the surface.

If you have a roll of dried up masking tape, don't discard it. Pop it in the microwave oven and cook it for 30 seconds. Once heated, the glue will soften and the masking tape will be sticky again. (Avoid using a microwave to cook food – it breaks down food molecules into toxic fragments that can have measurable impacts on your health. Treat your microwave as an industrial appliance only.)

You can also use cellotape, if you are sticking it to a non-painted surface, like plastic, chrome or rubber. Cellotape adhesive is strong and if stuck to a painted surface might pull off the paint if you're not careful. It might also leave some adhesive behind, which would need to be cleaned off.

Magic tape is a better proposition than either masking tape or cellotape. It is not as thick or irregular as masking tape. It also uses a gentler adhesive than either, so that it can be more accurately applied in a straight line or made to follow a curve. It's also less likely to pull off paint when you remove it.

Try to get as accurate or as straight a line as you can. You may need to pull some length of tape back off and re-apply. Be careful when handling masking tape that you don't pull it off vertically from the surface. Always pull off any tape at an acute angle, that is, as horizontally as you can. And slowly. You don't want to lift any existing paint if you can help it. And make sure that your masking materials are taped together without any gaps.

Use a wooden or plastic rule or better still, one of those bendy ones to help you with that straight line. The bendable plastic rule can follow any curves or contours without difficulty.

Chances are you will have your garage or shed open to allow for fresh air while you paint. Modest openings are a good idea. Allow for the occasional gust of breeze to upset the masking sheets, and use more tape for masking them down than you think necessary.

No Sway When You Spray

If you're spray painting small parts, you know that you can hang them up using old coat hangers and so have access for painting all the sides. This does not prevent the parts from swaying in a breeze or from the push of your paint spray. Not being able to touch the parts when they are wet with paint means it can be difficult to make the parts behave and stay still. Swaying is for dance floors, not for painting hanging parts.

One refinement you can do that cures this hassle is to use masking tape on the hooks of the coat hangers. Apply it where they are attached to a frame or overhead beam, etc. This way, any slight pressure on the hanging parts will not sway them away from your spray.

Thinners for Covers

If your vehicle has rubber splash covers in or around the engine bay and they were painted or undercoated, you can prepare them by wiping them down with lacquer thinners to remove any silicone off the surface. This will make paint adhesion a sure thing.

Be a Grounded Person

A grounded person is recognised as 'having their feet on the ground' and being a well-balanced person. You too can be a grounded person, at least as far as spray painting your vehicle is concerned.

Ground the body by wrapping a chain or heavy cable around the rear axle and letting it ground to the floor. This sees off any static electrical charge that may build up from the spray painting process. Always choose spray painting on a dry day if you can.

Keep a Count of Coats

During the painting process, you can keep a count of the coats you have applied by using a marker on an inconspicuous edge underneath the body. Use a gate-post counting method. You will also have an idea of how many coats and therefore how much paint can be removed in the colour sanding process.

Perfection through Professional Paint Partnering

I call it 'paint partnering' where you partner with an auto spray painting professional. You may choose to do all the preparation work up to the first coat of primer. You may choose to do some of the initial colour spraying and block colour sanding and leave the final coats to the pro. You may limit yourself to the panel metal work only, or the dismantling of mouldings, badges and other parts.

Either way, consider your costs and budget, including the expense (and risk) of transporting your vehicle from your garage to the paint shop. A professional spray booth has some measure of climate control, including dust filtering, heating for baked enamels and so on. Remember that a properly prepared vehicle (which you can do) is more than half the effort needed to arrive at a great paint finish.

Then there is the cost of the spray gun to consider. A cheap one won't cost a lot but will disappoint every time, compared with a professional quality device and the consistently good results it's capable of.

You will also need a good capacity air compressor which will not insinuate an aerosol of its own oil into the paint you spray! If you don't already have access to good equipment and a reasonable place to work in, like a well-ventilated garage or shed with adequate work space, you will need to consider whether you will be undertaking a lot of spray painting hobby work. If yes, then proceed with obtaining quality equipment. If it's a one-off, then of course, seek a Professional Paint Partnership.

Repairing, preparing and spraying even a single body panel to the required standard takes a lot of time, effort and commitment, although materials costs can be modest.

The problems of painting a car and the techniques to overcome them would require another book to cover adequately. That's not the e-book you are scrolling through now.

When I set out to write this e-book, I decided to limit myself to covering techniques and tasks that do not require extravagant equipment, facilities and costs. Spray painting a whole automobile or truck body approaches that limit, if not exceeding it altogether.

So I leave you with this concept of Professional Paint Partnering. Your efforts as detailed here in preparation and colour sanding, coupled with a professional paint booth and tradesman is, I believe, the best compromise for low-cost car restoration.

Post-Painting Filing of Edges

Once you have finished with your painting you will notice a build-up of paint around the edges of holes for things like badges, door handles and so on. If you attempt to re-install these objects, the squeezing in of them may chip off some paint from the panel edges.

Use a small hand file like a rat-tail file or a nail file, and carefully file away the excess paint material. Use only a pushing action when filing because a pulling action will chip the paint.

Wash Your Nylons

Nylon's good not just for stockings. Washers made from nylon, plastic or even rubber can be used when you're replacing a panel back onto the body. When you're adjusting the panel to a good fit (or a perfect fit if you're a perfectionist), the minor moving around can scrape paint off the mounting flange where your bolt and washer will attach. The washer is bound to have a sharp edge or two and few paints can resist a backward and forward metal-to-metal contact.

When you've aligned the panel and finger-tightened all the bolts into place, remove one bolt at a time and replace the nylon or plastic washer with the proper metal one. Tighten to the required torque and move on to the next one. Ensure there's no movement of the panel when you do this.

You can buy a selection from a rubber parts store or even at a home hardware chain. But it's likely that you probably have a handful of odd ones already in your small parts box or boxes.

Use the Card Guard

If you disassembled your vehicle by removing panels or doors there is a way to protect the paint when you are manhandling the panel or door back onto the body. (For those girls doing their own thing with their cars, we can say 'personhandling' but somehow it's just not the same.)

Use sheets of cardboard at least a foot by a foot (30cm by 30cm) in size and place them in the gap between the panels, or between the door and rocker panel underneath. Tape them in place to interior panels or surfaces where the tape itself won't lift paint when removed.

Now you can move and adjust your door or panel without the likelihood of scratching the paint off by accident. The cardboard sheet will also help in adjusting a consistent gap between panels or door.

Post-Painting Colour Sanding

You have done the deed with spray gun, thinners, masking and hopefully not much need for cursing. Most paints give an adequate shine 'off the gun' but nevertheless leave unsightly imperfections like an orange peel texture.

Whether it's your own work or a professional paint job, you can finish it to a higher standard with a final polishing using the block-sanding method. Ask the professional how much time is needed for the paint coats to cure completely before sanding. Apart from the directions on the can, a store person at the paint shop would be happy to impart advice too.

If the paint is lacquer, then three days should be allowed until block colour sanding can begin, then about six weeks before final polishing. Cold climate readers are reminded to let that six weeks go by with the vehicle indoors.

If the paint is a polyurethane, it must be colour block sanded WITHIN 48 hours after painting, but final polishing must wait for two months ideally.

If it's acrylic enamel (with urethane hardener) it's similar to polyurethane.

When the paint coats are ready, take out your sanding blocks. As mentioned before, offcuts of wooden two-by-four timber can be used in the place of hard rubber sanding blocks.

Wrap a 1200-grit wet and dry sandpaper around the sanding block and begin a section at a time. Clean the buildup of polish off the sandpaper with water. Dip it into a bucket of water, which you have placed so that you won't knock it over if you get up or stretch your legs. This sandpaper colour blocking will be sufficient to remove the orange peel. Do not press – move the block lightly and evenly.

Either way, you must sand the colour before the paint cures. This allows the top surface to breathe out the remaining solvents like the thinners in lacquer quicker than otherwise.

Ensure that you tape and mask off the interior and all the gaps to stop your polishing compound from entering unwanted areas.

Post-Painting Polishing

Wrap your wooden block with a clean rag so that the cloth surface is flat against the wooden surface. Think of it as a flat layer. If the cloth is too thin, wrap another layer around the block, being even more careful to keep the surface flat.

Use a light polishing cream and apply it with your cloth-wrapped sanding block. Be aware of how many coats of paint have been applied, how much paint you may have removed in the block sanding stage, and therefore how much paint you can afford to remove in the block polishing process. Depending on how deep the paint is, you can use a cutting compound paste that will give you good results sooner.

You are basically block sanding but at a much finer level, using polishing pastes rather than sandpaper. The polish is applied by cloth with a hard surface behind it. You are eliminating the final ripples or texture in the paint. Ensure your offcut is large enough to overlap several waves of ripple, so that you can polish the peaks down closer to the level of the troughs.

Use a backwards and forwards action, and then turn the movement at right angles to the original direction.

You can take this as far as you wish to go until you are satisfied with the result. Just check your work from time to time in good lighting and live with the result for a while.

Polishing the Pre-Existing Paintwork

Say you've just bought your car and would like to restore the paint finish, or had it for a long time and at last are ready to spend some time and effort on the paint.

If you don't have an electric buffer, not to worry. You can wax and polish by hand, using elbow grease. Change your arm, change body positions and exercise both your arms equally. It's great for both boys and girls as a muscle toner for upper body/shoulder definition. Wax on and wax off! Gym work and beautifying your car. Who said multi-tasking can't be done by guys?

If you are polishing aging paintwork, you must first thoroughly clean the body using a wax and tar remover. Working over a section at a time, polish any rough or oxidised panels or areas with a 1200-grit wet-and-dry sandpaper and lightly sand the rest with 1500-grit paper. Use sanding blocks as described above for a flat, even coverage.

Follow up with a cutting compound paste and then with a fine liquid polish. Use plenty of light including spot lamps to follow your progress. Waxing is the last stage, to seal in your paint's new lustre.

This does take time and when you are at the later, finer stages, it is important to keep dust and grit off the surfaces you are polishing and waxing. When doing the whole vehicle, give the next panel you will be doing a quick wipe down with a damp chamois cloth. This will pick up any dust or fine particles that have settled there while you were polishing or waxing elsewhere. This lessens the chance of scouring the paintwork with these particles and ending up with that annoying 'swirl' paint finish.

While waxing and polishing, prevent boredom. Note your progress from panel to panel and edge to edge across your car's surfaces, but you can also listen to music while doing so. Put your favourite radio station on. Set up your laptop nearby, provided that it's in a spot protected from sun, rain and dust. Listen to a YouTube talk where you'll learn something. However, if it's too deep, you may need to stop your waxing and let the implications sink in. The deep stuff is perhaps not recommended if it distracts you from your task.

Talk to a friend who's come by and is sipping a coffee (or with a beer in hand) is otherwise watching you work. A thoughtful friend will soon offer to help. If you ask him or her to 'give you a hand' and they clap, that's not classed as 'help'.

Even better, with any repetitive work - especially working alone - you can clear your thoughts. Don't plan your to-do list or shopping expedition. Don't dwell on the thoughts that do drop in. Don't give them any emotional energy. Let them go by, like scudding clouds across a deep blue sky. These thoughts will soon disappear and leave you alone.

Now you're in a state of meditation...

'Chop the wood', say various Eastern spiritual masters. Humble and repetitive tasks like chopping wood and fetching water can be made into a meditation. There's no need to chant 'om' or sit in a lotus position.

(My next book might be titled *'Zen and the Art of Car Restoration.'* Surely no one has written anything like it before!)

Avoid hard buffing where panels have edges or creases. You may take the colour coat off and discover the colour of the undercoat by accident. Save that detail work for later, with care and alertness.

Once the wax or polish is dry and powdery it can be removed easily with an open weave cloth, like cheese cloth. A white build-up of product will be seen around the edges of badges, lettering, pin-stripes and other raised edges. Simply use an old toothbrush to brush off this residue. (Save another old toothbrush for dirtier work involving the engine bay and other mechanicals.)

Anti-Chipping Stripping

No, this is not a burlesque show in a good cause. It's a way of preventing damage to your body paint (and no, I don't mean body paint for a Mardi-Gras parade or something, so get your head out of the gutter this minute).

When auto styling started to scoop away the under-body panels, it left them vulnerable to stone chipping from debris flying off the front tyres. Mud flaps could partly solve this problem, but not every car or truck was fitted with them.

Later, the radiator grille became less prominent and covered less of the front of a car as more front sheet metal became painted and vulnerable to flying stones from passing vehicles. Think of a 1970s Lincoln and recall that apart from the grille and bumpers, all else was painted sheet metal. Even the headlamps had eyelids.

Later still, the last vestige of the grille was removed to a place underneath the front bumper, in the underpan. This made more sense, as there was more cooling air to be got down there at higher pressure. The 1963 Studebaker Avanti was an early forerunner of this styling trend. This also exposed the front sheet metal to abrasion via stone chip after stone chip. Many sleek shovel-noses and drooping hoods fell victim to this onslaught.

Unsightly bug screens aren't the answer. These won't save doors and side panels anyway. Frequent re-spraying isn't either, particularly if you are dealing with hard-to-colour-match metallic paints. Mud flaps can prevent further damage, but not for the front of a car.

One solution that has been around for a while is the urethane film, made by 3M and others. These films are thinner than they used to be, so are more flexible. They are transparent and self-adhesive.

Lightly tape the film with its backing to the body panel. With a whiteboard marker (that can be wiped off) trace the outline of the area you want to protect. Remove the film and cut it out to that pattern.

Spray the recommended solution onto the panel to be protected. This would be a mixture of 75% water and 25% isopropyl alcohol, with a drop of dishwashing detergent to make the application easier.

Peel off about 2"-3" (50-75mm) of paper backing and apply the film to the wet panel, moving it as needed to its exact position. Slowly pull all the backing off.

Using a plastic or hard rubber squeegee, lightly squeeze out the water and any trapped air bubbles, working from around the centre of the film outwards.

Of course, it's a good idea to film over a painted panel that's already presentable. If stone chipped, all the chips should be touched up with paint to your satisfaction. Leave plenty of time for the solvents to outgas from the paint repairs – several days preferably, longer if they get wet. You're hermetically sealing it under the film. If a panel was professionally resprayed, ask the tradesman how long to wait before applying the film. He'll tell you, based on the number of coats applied, the type of paint and its out-gassing characteristics given the local climate.

Some films are even paintable. Check the manufacturer's instructions. In any case, the film will protect the painted panel from scuffing and stone-chipping and should stand years of abrasion before needing replacement.

Soap for Stripes

If you are applying decals or body stripes to complete your restoration, the best time to apply them is after you have colour-sanded or buffed and polished the paint, but before any wax has been applied. You are after the smoothest surface, but one free of oils and wax. Use a wax and tar remover first, ensuring that no oils from your fingertips are left over.

When you are ready to apply the decal or strips, use plenty of soapy water on the surface. This makes it easy to move the decal around until its position is perfect.

Windscreen Scratches

Always renew your windshield wiper blades. Never allow them to wear down to the base. It might be plastic or it might be metal. Sooner or later, something hard on your windshield wipers will come into contact with your windscreen glass. When this happens, scratches will follow.

Another thing you can do at the wreckers' is remove windshield wiper blades or assemblies from similar cars to yours and use these, but for the time it takes and the cheapness of the blades themselves, just buy the new ones and fit them yourself.

If you have a pre-existing scratch, buy some Jeweller's Rouge from a jeweller. It's an abrasive paste, originally coloured red (hence the name) and is designed to polish out scratches on glass. You can use this on your windscreen.

Let's say that you have a wiper arc scratch you want to polish out. Start from the bottom corner, near the windscreen edge. Apply your jeweller's rouge according to your jeweller's instructions and polish away. Keep a clean rag to wipe your work frequently and to check your progress. You want to avoid hazing the glass rather than removing the scratches.

As you gain skill, move up the arc and across the windscreen. Remove the jeweller's rouge completely when you stop, lest the abrasive travels to the paint or other places where it's not wanted.

Do this work in as much natural light as possible, or under a lot of incandescent light.

Avoid fluorescent light. It's bad for the eyes. The flicker is visible to your parasympathetic mind and is an irritant, together with the weird colour spectrum. As a result of fluorescent lighting, indoor office workers contract skin cancer, in places sometimes where no light reaches. Remember, sunlight good. Incandescent good (including quartz halogen). LED fair (if not blue). Fluorescent bad. Avoid whenever possible.

Pay for the extra electricity and use those quartz halogen filaments in a regular bulb. They're more efficient than the standard incandescent filament. And your body will be healthier and happier.

Eventually, you will reach a point where the scratch is difficult to see. Success! You've saved the expense of a new windscreen and the installation labour costs. And possibly some minor damage resulting from a windscreen replacement, if the tradie had scratched some paint or dented a moulding.

Keep a spare wiper blade in the trunk, just in case.

Window Seals' Secret Support

With all your side windows that raise and lower, they run past a rubber seal strip at the top of the panel. This strip prevents an excess of water from running down the glass and into the door or quarter panel. With all that exposure to ultraviolet light from the sun, even the best synthetic rubbers for outdoor use will deteriorate. This shows in the appearance of cracks, sometimes across the width of the strip and sometimes along its length. Sooner or later, two cracks will meet and a piece of the rubber strip will disappear forever.

Replacing these strips is usually a hassle, as it will require removal of the interior lining of the door panel and there may be further uncomfortable movements and contortions before the damaged strip can be freed and replaced with a new one.

You can buy lengths of the appropriate strip from an auto rubber parts supplier and hold it for the time when you will be doing other things inside the doors. This could be a clean out of dust and grit followed by any rust treatment or dousing of the insides with a 'wax-oil' to stop the spread of rust. Or it could be to grease the window raising/lowering ratchets or to replace electrical switches.

Whatever the occasion, you can use it to also replace the worn window rubber seal strip. But in the meantime...

Just lower the window into the door. Take some duct tape and affix it inside the vacant window slot, so that it will attach to the inside of the external window seal strip. You may have to clean the back of the rubber strip with a rag that is damp with thinners first, to ensure adhesion.

Raise the window glass and press the seal strip against it. This is pressing the duct tape on the inside of the strip between the glass and the seal strip, ensuring a better adhesion to the inside of the strip. Lower the glass window into the door and trim off any excess of duct tape so that it is level with the rubber strip edge.

You now have an extra backbone for the rubber strip which will prevent cracked fragments from falling off. This repair will last until you attend to something else within the door. Water does affect the adhesive in duct tape over the long term, but this method buys you some time. Incidentally, you can do this with the inside rubber seal strip too. It's not affected by as much exposure to water, so will last a lot longer.

Clean Your Plenum

If the vehicle has been parked under a tree, it will have collected a great deal of leaf and twig debris, which can find itself in a variety of unexpected places. Always remove the odd bit of leaf or other vegetable matter from the grille next to the windscreen. This leads to your interior air intake below. That's called a plenum, which is simply a hollow space. While there is usually a filter that air has to pass through before entering your interior (via the air-conditioning system), there is no fine filter at the outside grille to keep fine debris and leaves out.

When doing other tasks around the engine bay, you may consider removing the grille plenum panel behind the hood (and in front of the windscreen). This is usually secured with sheet metal screws or bolts. Once you have removed this panel (and probably the windscreen wipers first) take a moment to clean it out with a rag and detergent. You may even use the vacuum cleaner with a thin slot attachment to get into any seam or crevice where you see fine leaf litter accumulating. When it gets wet, this fibrous material stays wet and may be the starting point for rust in a most inconvenient area.

Whatever you can't pick up with the vacuum (or a long-bristled brush) can have its rust-promotion neutralised by spraying or brushing in some fish oil or similar rust proofing agent. If the stuff is thin, you might even pour it in there. Just beware that all the water drainage paths for the plenum are clear. You may need to poke out debris here and there with long, flexible plastic things like cable ties, or pipe cleaners.

Lastly (while you're there) lubricate any working parts, such as hood release levers and windscreen wiper arm pivots. Grease the hood release, and use engine oil in a squirt can for the rest. Don't use too much. If any spills, wipe it now, before replacing the panel.

If you must park your vehicle under a tree, rig up a tarpaulin with bungee cords for guy ropes. The tarpaulin will provide shade for your car and some protection from rain but also from falling leaves and twigs. Tree sap and bird crap will also be prevented from disgracing your car and damaging the paintwork – the bird droppings especially as some have a strong alkaline content.

When washing your car, use a sponge to apply detergent water on the 'good bits'. That is, all the top and upper body panels in good condition. Use another sponge – usually an older one with missing corners – to wash the lower body. This may be the bottom half of the doors and sides underneath a moulding line and around the bumpers and undertrays.

Likewise, use two chamois cloths to mop up the water – one for the normal outside panels and one for the door jamb areas and odd parts where some grease or oily residue is unavoidable. Chamois hates oil and an older, ragged leather should be used to mop up water in these fringe areas.

PART 4. APPEARANCE ITEMS

Restoring Clear Plastic Badges

Those nice badges which show a proud coat of arms with 'gules' and 'lions rampant' or chickens argent and all that good stuff are nice pieces of heraldic design. Either clear plastic lenses or badge covers protect nicely detailed lettering, numerals or symbols picked out in a chrome or golden plating. Once the clear plastic becomes not so clear, the effect is marred.

Return it to former glory and make the heraldic ancestor of that car maker proud.

The plastic has been affected by ultraviolet light, which typically hardens and oxidises the surface, making it craze on a microscopic level. To the eye, it becomes like a gauze, somewhere between opaque and clear.

Use a little auto paint polish on this surface, Rub it down and see if an improvement has been made. If you're making progress, try a medium-cut polish and apply lightly. You will be removing the outer oxidised layer and revealing a newer, clear plastic underneath.

Take care not to rub off any exposed chrome plating which may surround the clear plastic. You may finish off with a nice car wax to ensure some measure of UV protection, or alternately, a plastic and vinyl protectant like '303'.

Experiment on a similar piece with applying a coat of clear lacquer, either turps based, or thinners based. It's a gamble here, as it may attack the plastic if applied too heavily. But you may find a good result which could be used to protect that clear plastic surface well into the future.

Restoring Clear Plastic Headlamp Lenses

Go carefully here, because this is a complete assembly, meaning the headlamp bucket, its wiring and the clear lens. Only the globes and bulbs can be removed.

Now, you can go to your auto maker's spare parts division and pay a king's ransom (well, maybe a minor baronet) for a new one. Call your local wrecker's yard and ask whether they have the one you're looking for. The second-hand one may be in a better condition than yours. Then again, it may suffer from the same failing.

It may have gone yellow from exposure to ultra-violet in sunlight. Or there may be fine scratches or fine crazing on the surface.

For any of these problems try polishing your lens with a light polish for paint. The mild abrasive removes a microscopic top layer of the plastic, revealing the new material beneath. Fine scratches can be buffed out. If the yellowing is only skin deep, this too will polish out. Attempt this from the edges of the lens. As you are satisfied with the result, move across to the centre.

Some people recommend using bicarbonate of soda or baking soda as a light polish, with the option of adding toothpaste for extra cutting. Powdered limestone is used in toothpaste as an abrasive, apparently.

Finish off with a UV protectant like '303' (remember, no silicon oil). Sometimes you can fill in fine scratches with auto wax.

If any amount of polishing is not making a difference, or the scratches are too deep, then give it up and move on. Some things can be brought back, others not. You have to know when to cut your losses. That's a life skill too, and you learn it with other tasks and relationships.

Repairing Chrome Trim

The spray paint has not yet been invented that looks like a chrome plating. Some have tried, I don't think anyone has succeeded. Silver is a poor substitute for chrome. But here's a way to chrome plate without the plating.

Go to your local craft shop or online supplier. Buy yourself a sheet of chrome film sheet. This is an adhesive backed paper with an actual chrome plated plastic layer. It can be cut and scored with an Exacto knife of sharp Stanley knife, also a hobby scalpel. I have had a strip of this on an outside rubbing strip and it has still kept its shiny chrome finish.

Chrome has disappeared from this decorative strip on a Celica door. The white plastic is dull compared to the safety lamp bezel.

You will need a cutting board or sheet and a metal rule. The cutting sheet is useful where it's marked with measurements and a grid for right angles.

Measure the chrome moulding that you want to repair. If it's straight, as in a highlight strip on a rubber door rub strip, it's easy. If the surface to be covered in chrome is curved in cross-section, you will need to account for some extra width. Use a piece of paper to measure the curved cross section by following its curve from edge to edge. This gives you a realistic idea of the width you will need. Give yourself a margin for error, too.

With a sharp enough blade, you will be able to do your final cut *in situ*, without removing the rubber strip from the car.

Next, peel off the backing as you go, and apply the chrome strip to the plastic part of the rubber moulding. Ensure you keep it as straight as possible. Stick down the edge facing the middle of the strip (the rubber part). Leave the outside edge sticking out from the curvature of the moulding.

Definitely an 'after' photo. Application of chrome sheet has returned the trim back to its original lustre.

Now use a super glue. I do not recommend an all-purpose household glue or epoxy glue as this has 'body' and will not flatten completely after it's squeezed, so leaving a wavy surface for your chrome strip. Apply the super glue over a small length of strip at a time, then hold the chrome strip down to the moulding surface and wait for it to set. Do this for the whole length of strip. Smear the super glue over the whole width of the chrome strip you are applying. Its own adhesive won't be enough to keep it from curling off the curved surface of the moulding.

When it is set, go back with your Exacto blade or hobby scalpel and carefully cut between the body panel and the rubber moulding. There will always be a gap, no matter how fine. Take all the care you need here as you don't want to scrape off paint.

If you can do so, tuck in the edge of the chrome strip under the moulding and between it and the body panel. This tightly tucked curvature may place extra strain on the glue, so consider simply cutting the excess to match the original chromed edge.

Various auto interiors used chrome plated plastic strips to lend a bit of sparkle to a design theme. In the 1950s and 1960s, these were chromed steel or polished stainless steel. By the 1970s, chromed plastic was the order of the day. This has a much shorter life before the plating peels off or otherwise disintegrates.

This method lets you renew these strips and make them good as new, bring your interior up in presentability.

For added life on exterior applications, you can experiment with brushing a clear lacquer over a test piece of chrome sheet. If you're satisfied with the result, you can use it as an added layer of protection of the chrome against the vagaries of weather, wear and tear. Do this only with externally applied chrome sheet.

Turn Signal and Brake Lamps in a New Light

While we're on the subject of brightware, turning/running lamps and tail/brake light clusters are sometimes edged in chrome. Or if not, at least they have bright, shiny, reflective surfaces inside. Diecast hasn't been used for lamp assemblies since the 1970s, so most assemblies extant these days are plastic.

If the chroming has peeled off part of the housing, some people advise to spray paint it black. I think this is so 1980 that I won't even bother going there. For chrome repair, see the advice above for repairing chrome trim. For tiny damage, see advice below for restoring chromed badges.

In any case, unscrew the plastic lenses and remove them from the light assembly. Inspect the condition of the sealing gasket. Is it broken or brittle?

Has it let in water or dust? Clean out the interior of the lamp with a dry rag. If it's chromed inside, you may want to spray some WD40 or similar moisture barrier and wipe it around. This should prevent (further) corrosion. Remove the lamp bulb(s) and check the sockets for corrosion also. Do the same there.

Excess rust should be wire brushed out of the socket first. Use steel wool if the brush won't fit inside.

If the inside reflector surfaces of the lamp assembly are plastic painted silver, and the paint has become quite dull, you can carefully mask and respray with silver to brighten the lamp output. Or you can use aluminium foil or Bare-Metal Foil as described in 'Restoring Chromed Badges'.

To repair the gasket, use a silastic or silicon compound such as a gasket maker type, which is coloured black. Apply a bead to the mating surfaces of the gasket, lens and lamp housing. Press together and screw into place. If any oozes out, you can wait until it hardens before cutting off the excess.

The new gasket will take about 24 hours to fully cure.

You may want to use the gasket-maker to also seal the rubber boot that seals the entry point of electrical wiring into the lamp assembly. This is particularly so if the lamp cluster is in an exposed position under or outside the vehicle or where water may be splashed into it from a wheel arch. Some heat-shrink tubing may do the job there, too.

Restoring Chromed Badges

If you are recovering a badge or more complex surface, it would be best to remove it from the vehicle, so you can hold it in your hands and turn it over. Small things are done best on the kitchen table, wouldn't you agree? (Your partner might not. Never leave your work there. Always clean up after yourself. And kiss your partner for her (or his) forbearance.

Sometimes, cutting a stencil out of cardboard or paper may be needed to get the right shape. Then transfer it to your chrome sheet by tracing or cutting around the outline. Once you've placed the result over the badge and you're happy with the fit, place super glue on the badge surface, peel off the adhesive backing on the chrome sheet and place it on the badge, pressing firmly from the middle outwards. Make sure the glue reaches to all the edges. You don't want it curling up at these edges.

This only gives the top surface a chrome finish, not the edges, if it's a chunky badge. Pre-paint the edges with a chrome paint or a silver finish. These won't look as good, but will be much less noticeable when the highlight is the main surface and it's suddenly in chrome again. I would hazard a guess and say that no one would notice.

There are businesses now which can chrome plate plastics and in fact, anything. Pot metal, stainless steel…even leaves, for instance. You may not want a chrome plated leaf, but it does show what is possible with vacuum metalising. For the fastidious who want a restoration done just right, this is the solution. I believe that it's possible with mail order, so your location is not so important.

For some special locations, where the amount of 'chroming' is very small and not on a wearing surface such as a pushbutton, then I recommend 'Bare Metal Foil'. This is a handy product for plastic modellers to duplicate a chrome finish on model cars. It's a polished aluminium foil with an adhesive backing. It cuts with a scalpel, peels off the backing and can be laid onto a surface, burnished smooth with the tip of a cotton bud (or 'Q-Tip'). The adhesive is quite gentle, as the foil tears easily, being only a thin foil.

But the results are superb. If it works for modellers on model cars, it can work in out-of-the-way spots on the real thing. It costs a few bucks a sheet from hobby suppliers, and should be able to be mail-ordered from them.

For raised chrome edging on instrument panels or centre consoles, or even instrument panel lettering and such small features, this is better and easier than brushing on silver paint. With the scalpel, and some care - you can cut straight lines, something more difficult to do when you're painting freehand.

Naturally, the foil remains delicate, and can easily be scratched off or damaged. If you want the result, but anticipate the possibility of it being scuffed off, apply it, then when you are satisfied, use a small brush (the good sable one) and apply a coat or two of clear gloss lacquer over it. Once dry, the foil is sealed and protected from harm.

Chroming - Pro and Con

Chromium plating needs a lot of shop room and strict disposal procedures so is out of reach for the do-it-yourselfer. Kits are available for the hobbyist to nickel plate small parts, and this might be useful if there's a lot of nickel plating for bolts and fasteners and so on.

So – to chrome plate or not to chrome plate? You're coming back to the questions you asked yourself at the beginning of this e-book: how much time and resources do I want to spend; what results do I want to achieve; and why?

If you go all out on a 100% paint job and replace chrome bumpers or trim where the plating has been worn away, it will stand out horribly. On the other hand, if you have perfect plated parts on a car where the paint colour has faded or worn through to the undercoat in places, that will look unbalanced too.

Stainless steel trimmings can be carefully removed, have dents chased out and polished by a good professional. Chromed surfaces can be cleaned and waxed so that they shine and small imperfections will only be visible close up.

If the tiny pits and bubbles on a chromed cast headlamp rim on your classic car is in keeping with a sound but not perfect exterior, it can actually make for an authentic appearance. The so-called 'patina of age' in a classic or old car is becoming increasingly recognised in international circles as a valuable thing in itself. It marks an originality that can be lost after a concours-level restoration. The paint may be subtly faded; the leather seats marginally cracked but not broken and still supple enough to use; and the chrome bumpers and trim slightly pitted but without obvious dents or damage. Depending on the make and model, such a classic car may have as much market value as a 100-point fully restored *concours d'elegance* winner.

So if once cleaned and polished, the brightwork on your car is acceptable to you and in keeping with the rest of car, you can leave it as is. Small scratches can be coated by small brush with a clear lacquer to prevent rust or corrosion from getting a foothold. By regular cleaning and waxing you will halt or greatly reduce any further deterioration in your brightwork and it may outlast your ownership of the car or even outlast you!

All That Glitters isn't Chrome

To better understand chrome plating, we have to see it as a basically three-part process. First, the plater lays on a generous layer or two of copper, either soft or hard, depending on the original surface imperfections.

Then after polishing, a thinner plating of nickel is applied. This provides most of the mirror-like brightness, smoothness and corrosion resistance. A minimum of two layers of nickel is required for quality work – semi-bright nickel followed by bright nickel.

Finally, the thinnest coating of all is of chromium which gives that last unique 'blue' finish and high reflectivity to the surface. It's no more than several millionths of an inch in depth, so the surface must be as smooth as it needs to be before this last step.

Like other process described here, it is the foundations that make for the good result at the end. First, all the existing chromium, nickel and copper must be stripped off the part. Then all the scratches and blemishes must be polished out. The part must then be copper plated to fill in any small pits. The copper plated part must be buffed, cleaned and acid dipped, then rinsed and re-plated with copper. Nickel follows with the same method.

For best fit of your chromed parts and pieces, take them home with you at the initial copper plated stage. Small amounts of build-up of the part can be useful using the comparatively thick layer of copper plating. Temporarily attach the parts and inspect them for the right fit and gaps.

When you have your finished chromed parts back, take care in bolting them in. Particularly with bumper bars, if you neglect to use washers or bolt or screw the parts in too tightly, cracking can occur around the holes.

PART 5: WHEELS AND TYRES

The Menace of the Creeping Cover

Even if it sounds like the title of a bad 1950s sci-fi movie, this menace is serious.

Full-sized hub caps (or wheel covers as they are more accurately described) are great to look at. Mostly fitted to American cars – or American-inspired cars - the golden age of the fancy wheel cover were the decades of the 1950s and 1960s. Wheel covers were sculptured and styled, no less than the rest of the dream machines of that time. Paint inserts were added or 'spinners' and badges might further dress up wheel covers.

Fabricated from stainless steel or chrome plated, wheel covers brightened the sides of a car, even without the full-width whitewall tyres that often gilded these lilies of the road. Only the very outer rims of the steel wheels beneath were visible, sometimes not even that. Cadillacs featured stainless steel wheel covers that covered the entire wheel – all the way from one side of the tyre to the other!

If you have a classic or older car with full wheel covers, sometimes a cover will 'creep' around until it challenges the structural integrity of the tyre stem!

A fix for this annoying and potentially hazardous problem is to attach a little tab onto the inside of the wheel where the cover's tangs grip it. The tab will prevent any further rotation of the wheel cover and protect the stem of the tyre valve.

This '55 Buick wheel cover shows the red-painted rim of the steel wheel beneath. Note the vulnerable tyre valve stem and dig that wide whitewall tyre!

Make the tab out of a small piece of metal or a hardy plastic like nylon. It should be about the thickness of a pencil and long enough to cross the inside surface of the wheel which the wheel cover tangs brace against. It should also have a flat surface the better to adhere to the wheel metal.

With a metal tab, you can spot weld it into place. An easier method is to use an epoxy glue, which can be applied to a tab made from any substance. Either way, scrape off all the paint from the place on the wheel where you wish to attach the tab. Remove just enough to allow for a good adhesion.

Here on this 1958 Sixty-Two Sedan, Cadillac introduces full-width wheel covers which hide the wheel completely. Compared to the other decorations (this was the Year of Chrome for GM makes) they look rather tasteful.

Mix the epoxy glue and apply it to both surfaces as directed on the instructions. Attach the tab to the steel wheel and line it up into place. This will be fairly close to the tyre valve stem. Ensure that the tab does not stick outwards from the wheel so much that it will interfere with the fit of the wheel cover when that is replaced.

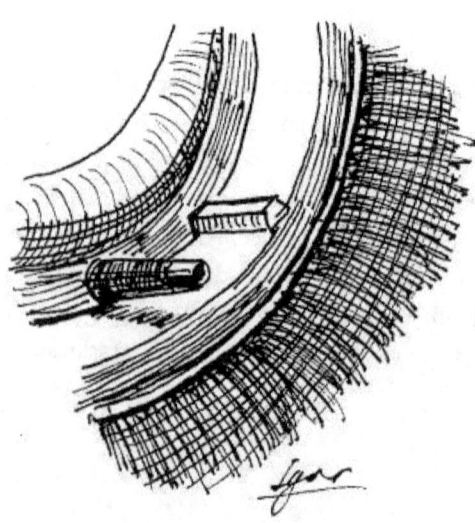

Allow the epoxy glue to set and dry to maximum strength.

Once you have waited the appropriate time, coat the tab and the bare steel wheel around it with a primer followed by a colour-matched paint. With a black wheel, this is easy, but a particular colour will need a close match so as to hide your little modification.

Allow to dry and then replace the wheel cover.

Wheeling and Cleaning

Since asbestos was dropped from the formula for brake pads and brake shoe linings, carbon has taken its place. This fine black dust mars the appearance of many open spoke type alloy wheels. It seems 'greasy' and difficult to remove.

To clean it, use a series of disposable paper towels; an old, long-handled scrubbing brush (used for nothing else) and straight detergent. Spray the detergent and scrub away – it's an unfortunate fact of life.

Most over-the-counter wheel cleaners are based on phosphoric acid – the stuff you drink in a cola soft drink. If you've run out of the real stuff, you can always wet a rag with 'the real thing' and wipe it over the dirty or rusty patches. Allow to dry and wipe the excess off. There's a lot of sugar there which may attract unwanted attention from ants.

If you have alloy wheels that are coated with a clear glaze, too strong an acid may peel this protective coating off. A strong alkaline degreaser may have the same effect. Ask at the counter of an automotive products shop for advice on the best product for your wheels.

For chipped or scratched steel wheels, rust proof then prepare and paint them if required to cover up scratches or chips in the paint. A spray gun or aerosol can is sufficient to do a good job. If you have an old style steel wheel that's mostly covered by a wheel cover, you can get away with brushing on a coat of paint. Take extra care with painting the rim not covered by the cover, as this will be visible.

And please take the time to mask the tyre off properly! It'll take less time than wiping off ugly overspray with solvent or abrasive cleaner from a damaged sidewall.

For polished alloy wheels, you may consider polishing them with a mild cutting polish and then prepping and spraying a coat of clear gloss lacquer over them. Some alloy wheels are unpolished but coated instead with a paint or clear coat. Repaint as desired. Instead of a grey coloured, alloy wheel paint, you could select a metallic grey. Or if you are custom mixing paint for a spray gun, you can choose a grey with a dash of silver. Ensure the covering is tough enough to serve on a wheel and colour matchable if you scuff the rim later on a kerb.

In any case, finish off by washing and waxing the wheels, whether they are steel or otherwise. A waxed surface is easier to clean, and wax also protects the chrome plating on a steel trim ring or hub cap. These are often neglected and are exposed to more moisture and road grime than other bright mouldings.

For mild pockmarks of rust spotting on chromed hub caps, wheel covers or trim rings, wipe down with a phosphoric acid based rust converter. Don't use steel wool or scouring pads on these chromed surfaces. The chrome is rather soft and will scratch. Use cloths or rags instead. Allow the rust converter time to dry then rinse off or wipe down with a wet rag. Once dry, wax the chrome to protect it.

Whitewall Tyres Scrub Up

Whitewall tyre bands can be cleaned with a kitchen powder cleanser like 'Jif'. Apply with a wet rag and scrub on, using another part of the rag to wipe off. I have had good results with a soft scrubbing pad, either of plastic, nylon or a very fine steel wool. The fine steel wool scrubbers are often impregnated with a soap, which lathers as soon as it's wet.

Scrub lightly and wipe off as you move around the tyre. Dirtier whitewall stripes may need a repeat application. Rinse off with water frequently.

Be aware as to whether you have a genuine whitewall tyre or one that has had the white stripe buffed and painted in. Some excellent whitewalling is available through mobile tradesmen who can transform the tyres you chose for their size and design into otherwise unobtainable whitewall versions. The white rubberised coating they apply won't go very deep into the tyre as a 'real' whitewall. Check this first before scrubbing with gusto.

PART 6: INVOLVING OTHERS AND A FINAL WRAP-UP

Spare Parts - Hunting and Gathering

This aspect of the restoration project was briefly mentioned in the context of gleaning interior parts in Vol. 1. It needs expansion here as it's so much more applicable to the quest for better body and mechanical parts. We can't grow our spare parts in an agricultural sense but we can go hunting and gathering to find them.

The richest pickings are found at a salvage yard. The pick n' pay type of junkyard is the best. It's cheaper because the staff aren't the ones removing parts from cars. Sort of like a self-serve wrecker's yard.

Get your girlfriend or wife to come with you to the wrecker's. Women LOVE shopping and this will trigger their 'hunting-for-bargains' neural circuitry. She'll catch on straight away to what you're looking for and help you find it. She won't even mind wearing old jeans and t-shirts and stepping into mud to help get that unusual part.

Now don't misunderstand me: your lady is not there to stand at attention and hand you a spanner, a screwdriver or a beer when you ask for it. She is there to hold the hatchback lid up or the door open while you squeeze in and unbolt something. Someone likewise to hold up that hood and to help solve problems. Not your servant, but your equal. (She knows this already, but it's nice if you acknowledge it).

She might also become more involved with the restoration project!

You enter the yard bringing your own tools, plastic bags, old newspapers, penetrating oil like WD40, hand cleaner and a written list. Then you go fossicking for the parts you need or might need. If it's a hot day, bring a small bottle of water. If rain threatens and you're not deterred, a second person makes a handy umbrella holder.

Back to the wrecker's yard. Depending on public liability insurance clauses, the yard may be able to stack cars one on top of another. If not, they will all be at ground level. Something about a member of the public not falling off the car on top and suing for injuries.

Use the car underneath to climb up to the next one. Pick your footholds and hand-holds carefully. The cars in wrecker's yards seem to be liberally sprinkled with broken glass. At least this is toughened glass, which shatters into small pieces which generally do not have sharp edges.

The yards I've been to use the unfortunate method of moving cars around by forklift. The forklifts smash their forks through the windscreen and raise the car by the roof. They haul it around this way, by destroying the windscreen, roof panel and internal ceiling all at once. I suppose this prevents damage to the underside and mechanicals or other parts, but still seems a shame.

The other effect is that there is always broken glass in a car interior at these wrecker's yards. If you've found your part from a donor car, also make use of the time that you're there by removing nuts, bolts and screws, from the engine bay and interior. You may be surprised at how often an extra spare nut, bolt or other fastener may come in handy. They can disappear while you're working; fall down an inaccessible crevice down the engine bay; break; have bad threads or rounded heads.

Domestic Car Restoration Etiquette

Clutter creates stress… irritation … can lead to arguments and flaring tempers.

Separate where you live and where you work. Car restoration may be a necessary chore to save money or improve your ride. It may be total play for you, but it can get as filthy as any work can. If you take your mechanical work indoors, prepare first-hand with old newspapers or other protection for surfaces you might otherwise eat off or rest cutlery on.

When you're finished, or when it's time to stop, repack all your parts in the small tray or box you carried them in and carry them out. Put away your tools and products and clean up after yourself.

Indoors car restoration should be done in moderation. Don't do something stupid like cleaning a transmission in the bathtub. Heavy castings with sharp edges will chip and damage the bath enamel. You might also do your back in by lifting it in and lifting it out again. You'll also have a mess that's hard to clean - and harder to hide. Avoid this pitfall altogether.

Take Pity on Your Neighbours

One of the definitions of a 'redneck' is someone who mows the lawn and finds a car.

Be neat with your visible property and be neat with your restoration projects or spare parts cars, if you have them. How? Simple.

Hide them.

Hide them in your backyard behind a high fence. Preferably under cover, as in a shed.

Under cover and out of sun and rain will help preserve your vehicles and parts, keeping their value to you and whoever might want to buy them. Look at your domestic junk and your car parts or cars, and what is stored inside and under cover and what sits outside. Which is worth more? Is it a choice between a lawn mower and a car? Think it through.

Hide your parts cars or restoration projects especially from the neighbours, who might complain to your local council. If you're doing stuff which is at the limits (or beyond) of what's allowed outside of an industrial area, be very kind to your neighbours.

You know that the best way to prevents neighbour's complaints about a noisy party is to invite them to it. I believe in this principle.

If they're so inclined, you can even invite your neighbours to help you out in your project. They may learn stuff themselves and might take enough of an interest in your project not to complain if you wake them up early on a weekend with an air compressor for your spray gun. Try not to do banging and loud stuff too early – or too late.

Throw a BBQ when you've reached a significant milestone and celebrate it with your neighbours. Proudly show off your work and how you did it. A mechanically finished and painted chassis and engine from a vintage car?

Show it off! No grille or mouldings yet, but you've done a new paint finish on your Finned Fabulous Fifties dreamboat? Show it off! If they don't become good friends, at least they'll be more tolerant.

When your ride is finished and on the road, offer to take the neighbours out for a spin. If their daughter gets to go to the Prom in your classic car or some such rite of passage, (such as getting married) they'll be more than delighted.

You've Finished - A Sense of Closure

Consciousness is found in our fellow humans, to a greater or lesser degree. Consciousness is also found within matter itself, so the mystics say.

Increasingly, quantum physicists are putting their hands up and agreeing. For consciousness cannot be separated from experimental results at the subatomic scale. It is theorised that below the sub-quark level there lies the quantum vacuum. This 'vacuum' is not empty by any means, being a medium that is super-dense with energy. The substrate under this in turn is the ultimate field. This foundation is made of nothing but information, and it spans the entire universe and permeates all things.

Why is this deep stuff in a book on car restoration?

I'll answer this question with some questions. What has been absorbed into or attached to the matter that is your car? Does it remind you of an unpleasant time? Does it bring memories of a troubled relationship?

If so, it needs a 'clearing' or ceremonial 'blessing' to remove any negative energies or associations. It doesn't matter if you believe that it's just a lump of inanimate metal, plastic, rubber and fabric. Your ride is a thing of meaning. A car of dreams. A vehicle of memories. A transport of delight. It has meaning for *you*, otherwise you wouldn't spend so much time and effort on it, right?

Therefore, perform a ceremony of clearing / blessing / intention. Wipe away any bad associations with your conscious intent. Find and copy something and adapt it or invent a ceremony from scratch. They launch ships with bottles of champagne. Do something similar (go easy on breaking things on the hood though).

Mark the moment when the project is done – or largely done. Invite your friends. If they think you might be a bit eccentric, do it on your own. Perform it solemnly. Or act it out humorously. It doesn't matter which. Just do it with meaning and intent.

Chant a spell. Intone an affirmation. Imagine a protective aura of blue light around the car. Picture negative associations dispersing away like smoke, falling away like particles of rust. Ring a little bell. Recite a poem. Sing a song. Have sex in the back seat.

Do it all with the right intention. The intention that all negative connotations are wiped clean and it's a new start. (We started out by asking what your intention was and now we are finishing back with it.)

Consider it a small, extra task but a ritual well worth it.

May your restoration be low in price but high in satisfaction and reward!

Happy restoring and happier motoring!

PART 7: APPENDICES

Here's some bonus, extra-value information that you'll really appreciate having. You may even find it worth the whole cost of the book. Just sayin'.

APPENDIX A: TRADITIONAL MAINTENANCE

Remember the regular stuff. A car or truck is a machine, and a machine needs regular maintenance. This includes adjustments and changing working fluids. Here are some great tips.

Oil and Oil Filter

You can follow the recommendations of the automaker or filter manufacturer as to how many months of use (or non-use) or kilometres or miles of distance between oil and oil filter changes. Many people don't.

Just do that and you're already ahead of the curve. But you can go further.

With a normal 7,500 mile (12,500 km) oil and filter change interval, this is according to "normal" use, whatever that means. If you read further on the label or instructions, it gives the exceptions.

Oh, oh, the fine print. It says to change oil and oil filter more frequently (like 3,000 miles / 5,000 kms) under "dusty driving conditions, stop and go city driving, driving in heavy traffic in extremely hot or extremely cold conditions, or frequent short trips."

Most trips by motor vehicle are short, and inevitably involve being stuck in slow or stop-and-go traffic at some point. So it pays to change your engine oil and oil filter more frequently. If you're keeping the car, then you'll make it last longer and save money in the long run by spending a little more here and now. After all, spending twice as much on motor oil and filters can't compare with an engine overhaul, or even with the labour and expense of having a second-hand engine swap for your car.

Clean Your Machine

Wash your car or truck often. It reduces the time that dirt or bird crap spends on the paint, as the latter can mar paintwork like any alkaline attack. Make it at least once a month, more often if you can. If you're time poor, consider patronising a commercial car wash where they wash by hand. Wax your vehicle at least twice a year, more often if water stops beading on any outside surface.

Vacuum your interior monthly. Even if you drive with the windows up you'll be surprised at the amount of dust that intrudes into your car. Most interiors nowadays are cloth or velour rather than vinyl. Vinyl or leather seats can be wiped clean. Cloths trap fine abrasive dust, which can grind into the fibres when you plant your behind onto the seat. This goes for the carpets, too.

Vacuum first, as it raises dust. Then wipe your surfaces with a mild liquid soap or detergent. Dry it off with a clean rag or towel and finish with a wipe-down of a vinyl / plastic protectant dressing. Finish your interior with glass cleaning – the windscreen if nothing else, followed by the rear screen and all the side windows.

Spray some silicon lubricant or even squirt some drops of engine oil into the felt-lined channels that your windows travel up and down in. (See the 'Cleaning Your Interior' sub-chapter above for more details on interior cleaning.)

Replace your air-conditioner dust/pollen filter according to the recommendations. It's a replaceable paper filter, usually accessible from your interior.

Some cars with air-conditioning never came with such filters. My Rover 3500 SE apparently never had this. A makeshift is to save a plastic meat tray from a supermarket. Cut out the bottom of the tray and lay a thin layer of plastic sponge within, making sure it's sealed. Turn it upside down and place it over the air intake for the air-conditioner or heater. This may be inside your interior or outside, within the intake air plenum behind the engine bay. Attach it temporarily as best you can, with a view to being able to remove it easily later.

Lightly oil or spray the foam with a scented oil before a long trip, say with a eucalyptus oil or pleasant essential oil. This won't last but will give a pleasant fragrance to your interior. If you don't like the scent after all, change to another. I recommend peppermint essential oil, as it smells fresh and keeps you alert.

This sponge serving as the interior air filter is a stopgap measure, as the plastic foam may reduce the free flow of air into your car. Find a way to adapt a commonly available paper filter and its housing to your vehicle. Seal it around the edges as best you can with foam rubber strips or such. Note the make and model the filter element came from so you can replace it when needed.

With all your windows up and air entering through the heater/air-conditioner, don't import dust and dirt from outside if you don't have to!

Aromas to Please

A pleasant aroma inside your vehicle has several benefits – it can reduce the feeling of 'dead' air; and can help to keep you feeling fresh and alert. However, do you dislike the car deodorants you are forced to buy, with dispensers that stick out on your dashboard air outlet grilles or hang from your rear-view mirror? I know I do. I'd rather have something out of the way.

You can use a scrap of plastic sponge as a deodorant diffuser. Just cut it to a rectangular shape and place it under the dash near an air outlet, or within the heater/air-conditioner plenum, if this is easy to access. You might even have a thin sheet which can tuck under the driver's or passenger's seat. If there is air flow under the seat, the fragrance will still infuse the interior.

Attach the sponge with a plastic cable tie or hook or even a wire tie from a plastic bag for bread. Keep a small spray bottle in the car to atomise your essential oil or fragrance onto the sponge from time to time.

For the right fragrance or aroma, go to a health food establishment or a New Age type shop with crystals in the store window. Chances are they'll have a good range of essential oils to choose from and knowledgeable staff to help you with your choice. A tip for the boys: most of the customers are women and you might even pick up there. Just kidding.

Maintenance Logbook

Buy an inexpensive diary or booklet and make it your vehicle logbook. Record your oil and oil filter changes with columns for date and mileage. List your other maintenance actions. You'll have a better idea when planning ahead, as to when the next service action is due. You'll also be able to give your garage mechanic more facts when you approach them with a problem.

You might even note down any strange noises or impressions coming from your car and the mileage and date it occurred. If you know how old your battery is, or how often you've changed your fluids and filters, that might make diagnosing a problem easier. You'll also know how long something lasts before needing repair or replacement.

Photocopy or copy by hand your car's maintenance schedule from your owner's manual. Put it inside the back cover of your log book. It tells you the maintenance or inspection intervals and serves as a handy reminder.

Spark Plug Report

Check your spark plugs' gaps and condition at recommended intervals, more often if you do a lot of that "dusty driving conditions, stop-and-go city driving, driving in heavy traffic in extremely hot or extremely cold conditions, or frequent short trips." That could mean as often as monthly.

Something handy to do is to prepare a simple drawing of your engine block. You could do this on a page to go into a folder of all your car receipts, or if you can write small, you can do this on a page of your maintenance logbook.

Draw a simple outline of your engine. Then draw in a series of circles to show the positions of the cylinders. In a straight engine, all you need to do is to indicate which is the front or rear of your diagram, or left and right hand side if it's laterally placed in the car. With a vee engine configuration, I draw a simple top-down view. For example, to show a V8 engine, draw a rectangular outline and two rows of circles within. Draw where the steering wheel is in relation to the engine. This shows that the diagram represents the view when seen from above (and usually) from the front.

Now remove each spark plug and measure the gap, clean it as necessary and note its condition by writing brief notes around the outside your diagram. Use arrows to point your text to the appropriate cylinder/spark plug.

Is the plug oily? Is it coated with a dry black deposit? Is it a fine grey deposit? Is there a glazed part on the insulator? Is the electrode eroded? All of these features have something to say about the conditions inside that cylinder under the running you have been doing.

You will find a complete guide to diagnosing what your spark plugs have to say in every workshop manual, usually with full colour pictures.

By the way, buy a workshop manual – they are indispensible as guides for all mechanical work you can reasonably expect to undertake. If you have a common make and model of car, you may find used ones in a second-hand bookstore or at a stall on a major car club display day or parts meet ('swap meet' in Australia, 'auto-jumble' in Britain).

Before returning the spark plug, look inside the plug hole. What you see is part of the top surface of the piston. Short of using a medical optical diagnostic tool – the sort that's shoved down your gullet to inspect the condition of your stomach – you won't be able to see the entire piston face. However, just seeing a glimpse of part of it may be enough. Use a work light; a narrow one if you can, such as an LED cluster on a pen light or tiny flashlight. What do you see inside? Is the piston surface dry black or does it look oily? Does it have patches of dry black and patches of (relatively) clean aluminium?

Make notes as appropriate on your spark plug engine diagram. This too will give an idea of the status of each cylinder, helping you track down where oil is leaking past valve stems or worn piston rings. Is one side of your vee engine running richer than the other? The deposits on your piston surfaces or spark plugs will show. You don't even have to see all of the piston top to gain value from this diagnostic technique.

Once you have cleaned and re-gapped the spark plug as necessary, replace it carefully, so as not to introduce scale and dirt into the cylinder or on the plug thread. Tighten by hand to ensure the plug is on the thread properly. Sometimes it's difficult to see whether it's at the correct angle for engaging the thread. Go by feel and exercise patience. When you can hand-tighten no longer, finish tightening by socket. Use a torque wrench set to the recommended torque if it's not too bulky to use in your engine bay. Once you have done this exercise once or twice you will soon know how tight to go with your plugs.

Reconnect the ignition lead to the plug. Now move on to the next spark plug. Remove, inspect and clean ONLY ONE PLUG AT A TIME. It might seem more efficient to take them all out and clean and adjust them at the same time, but boy, if you get that ignition lead sequence wrong with just one mistake, your engine will misfire, or likely not run at all. Rather than memorising where all the spark plug leads go or labelling them all with numbered strips of masking tape, save yourself the hassle.

Do one plug service (and piston top inspection) at a time. Write your notes, then move to the next one. It has the added advantage of needing less time to be road-ready, in case you have to abandon your work for an urgent chore that requires your car.

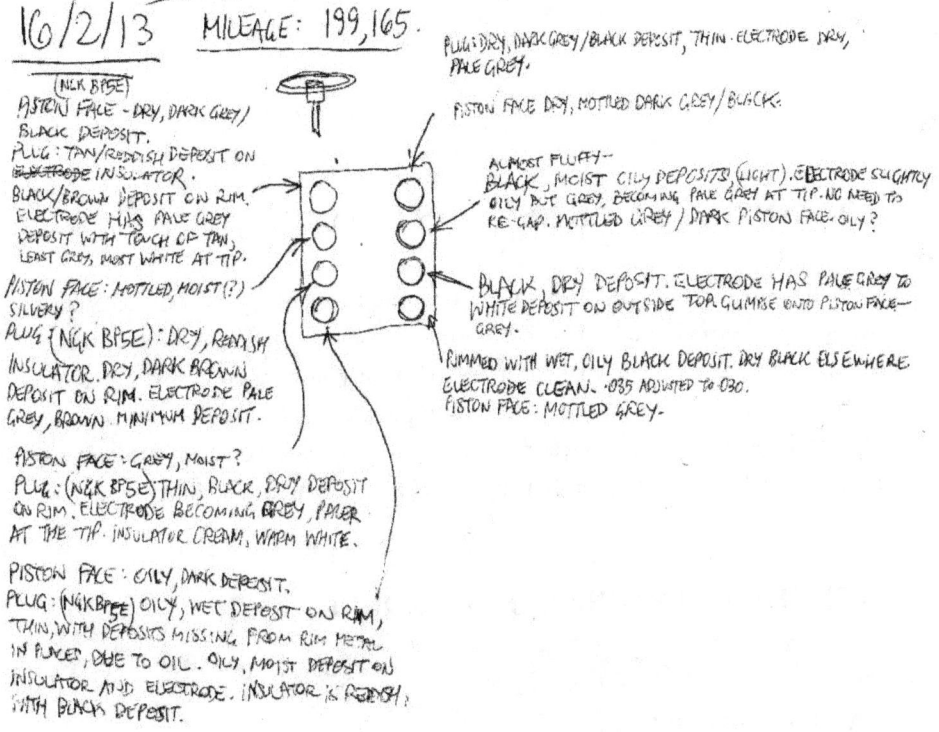

An example of a spark plug report. Nothing fancy is required, just a simple diagram and your notes.

APPENDIX B: EXTREME MAINTENANCE

This isn't like doing tune-ups in the nude or changing your oil while suspended from above like Tom Cruise in *Mission Impossible*. Whatever turns you on, but what I mean by 'extreme' doesn't involve sports. It's doing auto maintenance at the next level, where few people go. If you have your ideal set of wheels or a pricey investment in classic cars, and you're after extreme motor vehicle longevity, here's a suggested maintenance schedule.

WEEKLY MAINTENANCE SCHEDULE

Check engine oil level.

Record in your log book how much oil you add to offset loss through leaks or burning.

Check engine coolant level.

Always top up with more of the same coolant or antifreeze/antiboil additive, or top up with distilled water. Water from a domestic kitchen filter is quite satisfactory too as it has removed most impurities held in suspension in your tap water. Avoid adding tap water if you can. Especially avoid mineral-rich bore water. Use these only in emergencies.

Check auto or manual transmission level.

Top up as required. Note if you're losing auto transmission fluid. It usually means the oil pan gasket is the cause, but in any case, you'll know what to look for next time you crawl underneath for some other reason.

Check brake fluid level.

Top up as required. If you have to top up and there are no leaks, it is a sign that your brake pads and/or shoes are gradually wearing away. This is normal, but usually takes a longer while to be noticeable.

Check windscreen washer fluid level.

Add a detergent made for windscreen washers as desired.

Check battery electrolyte level (non-sealed batteries).

Top up with distilled water only. On sealed batteries, look at the colour of the 'eye' window.

Check condition of engine bay hoses.

Are they excessively soft or hard? Do they kink rather than curve? They probably need replacing.

Are they chafing against a surface at one point? Enfold them in a sacrificial layer of sheet rubber (see elsewhere in this edition).

I have seen a throttle linkage cutting little nicks out of an air-conditioner hose on the firewall. It was because the engine/gearbox mounts had deteriorated to the point that the whole assembly could move backward, far enough towards the firewall to cause this damage. With modern engine bays being packed so tightly with endless mechanical stuff, the gaps allowable before damage occurs have shrunk alarmingly.

Put it on your to-do list. An ounce of prevention…

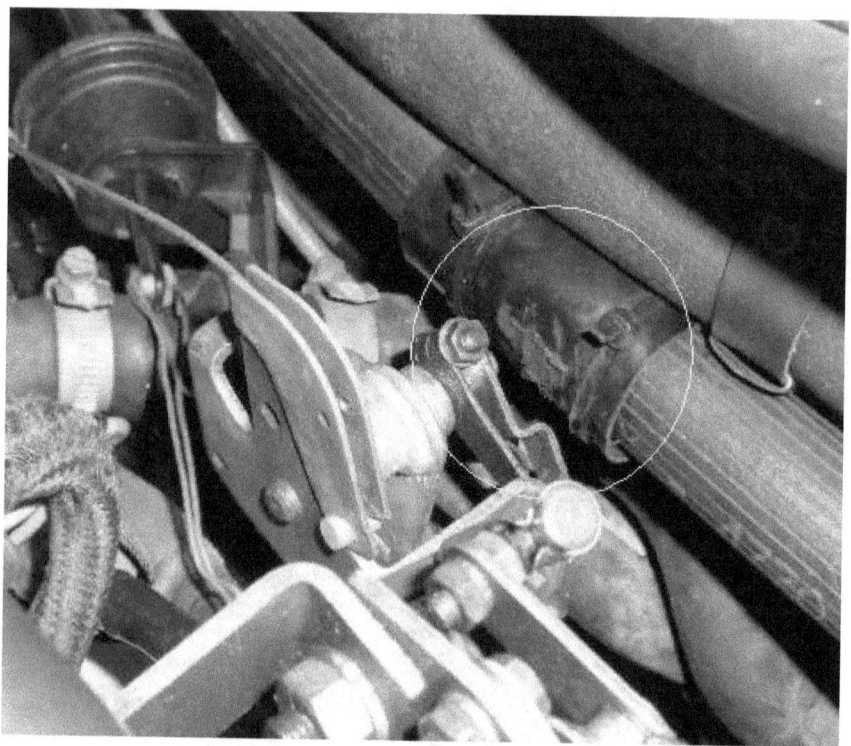

The air-conditioner hose has been wrapped with a sacrificial rubber sheet. Note the abrasion on the sheet (circled) caused by the throttle linkage nearby. If the air-con hose is punctured, then an expensive repair and re-gassing of the system follows. Move the wrapped sheet around to even out the wear until a mechanic can re-adjust or replace the engine mountings.

Check tyre pressure and tread condition.

Is one tyre losing air more than others? Does it have a nail embedded in the tread? How happy you are that we live in the age of tubeless tyres! Note it for later attention at your local garage at your convenience. Are the treads wearing unevenly? Organise a wheel alignment immediately. When was the last time you had a wheel alignment? Your logbook would tell you.

Allow about half an hour for these inspections.

MONTHLY MAINTENANCE SCHEDULE

The weekly schedule as listed above, and the following additions:

Lubricate all hinges.

Use a little can with the trigger–squeeze and long, narrow neck. Engine oil is best for the hinges for the larger panels, such as doors. If the hinges are completely enclosed with only tiny gaps then try a thin 'handy oil' or sewing machine oil. As it's thinner, it may seep into the cracks better and reach the hinge pin or rod itself. WD40 may eliminate squeaks, but it is not the best lubricant. Try spraying silicon lubricants if no oil can seep inside the hinge housings.

Lubricate the seat runners.

Do this with grease or engine oil. Try not to get any on the carpet! Don't use too much as it will attract dirt and carpet fibres. Wipe away any visible excess.

Lubricate throttle linkage.

Use oil sparingly, as you don't want to amass a deposit of oily dirt over these parts. If there's any binding, try a penetrating oil or WD40 first to clean it out, then oil it.

Test battery specific gravity.

This bulb horn with the glass tube and soft spigot may look more like a prop for Harpo Marx these days, but the hydrometer is useful for checking the specific gravity of your battery acid. This says how much charge and how efficient your battery is.

Batteries gradually lose their ability to store charge, and it's when you're cranking a cold engine in cold weather that a battery is put to the ultimate test and is most likely to fail to 'deliver the goods'. Monitoring your battery condition will allow you to plan ahead for its replacement, rather than suffering a rude shock and an unexpected cash outlay.

If your car has a voltmeter, this too will give you an idea of battery condition.

Lubricate ball joints.

If this is applicable and they aren't sealed forever, grease them. Suspension components take hard hits and deserve all the lube they're designed for.

Check spark plug gap and condition.

Record your findings as described above.

Check distributor cap, points and rotor.

Remember distributor points? Not many cars or trucks have them now. Electronic systems generally work by photoelectric cells that use light to synchronise ignition, without the spark machining that wears away the surfaces of points. They require no replacement, but sometimes plastics go brittle and crack. So inspect the rotor with this in mind. Make sure the distributor cap has no cracks either, as it may admit moisture inside. Moisture is antagonistic to both electrics and electronics.

Check fuel filter.

This is easy with a see-through type in the fuel line, or in a glass bowl at the base of a mechanical fuel pump. A non-transparent casing is trickier. Some in-line filter canisters are alloy and their insides impossible to evaluate. Also remember the high pressure that fuel is under when being ready to be sprayed by a fuel injector. If you disconnect a filter that is downstream from the fuel pump, you'll have an unpleasant experience involving copious amounts of petrol in all sorts of unwelcome areas.

Replace your fuel filter according to recommended intervals or more often if you've come across dirty fuel in the past. Ethanol in petrol can clean or scavenge some older debris from the bottom of your fuel tank and it ends up in the filter, which it's supposed to do. This means, though, that you have to be extra vigilant about replacing the fuel filter at least at the recommended intervals.

You might even consider carrying a spare fuel filter around.

Check air cleaner and filter housing.

Take out your paper filter element and knock it against a hard surface to loosen off any tiny dust and dirt. Make sure the filter edges are air-sealed by the filter housing. Replace the filter element more often if you drive in dusty conditions.

Some filter elements are made from plastic foam, with a metal mesh inside acting as a structural backbone. These elements are oiled with a proprietary oil and this combination makes for an unbeatable way of cleaning the incoming air. You periodically wash the elements in detergent, dry them and then re-oil them. The element is not disposable like a paper element and it never wears out.

One minor point is to not re-oil these filters by spraying on their special oil from a pressure pack. The hydrocarbon propellants are said to attack the plastic sponge. You can spray into a clean, shallow tray and apply the oil with a brush set aside for this purpose.

Check air cleaner thermostat.

Is it binding or moving freely? Are those big, silvered air hoses intact?

Check vacuum hoses for cracks.

You'll need lots of daylight or artificial light for this. Look around high heat sources first, such as the exhaust manifold or engine block. Consider hoses that have to make unusually sharp curves. Stress cracks may occur in areas where the hoses have to absorb vibration or movement. Keep a number of hose offcuts that match the ones your vehicle uses handy in your garage. Even if the offcuts are not long enough to replace a length of damaged hose, they are portable and can be used as size guides when buying a replacement.

Check weather-stripping, trim and mouldings.

Cracks or missing fragments in weather-strips or rubber window sealing strips? Keep an eye on their deterioration or you may find unwelcome weather intruding into your interior. Or worse, rust coming out in an unwelcome debut. (A low-cost repair method is described elsewhere in this edition.)

Is the trim held on by fewer and fewer attachment points? Grab some new or second hand brackets and replace the broken or missing mountings. If it's a small trim, you may be able to get away with double-sided tape, (though exposure to rain water may dislodge it sooner rather than later). Take action before your trim falls off the car, never to come home again.

Same goes for mouldings. These tend to be specialised pieces in either stainless steel, chromed metal, rubber or high-impact plastics. They'll usually be noticeably by their absence and will devalue your car and truck considerably.

You'll have the additional unwanted task of tracking a replacement down in a wrecker's yard or paying a sky-high price from a dealer for a new one. (You may be forced to buy an unwanted pair of mouldings!) That's if you can even find a replacement piece.

Save yourself the extra trouble – re-attach it at the first opportunity, properly if you can, temporarily if you must.

Vacuum your seats and carpet.

Shampoo your carpet. Fight that abrasive dust that naturally finds its way into any vehicle, and can cut through the fibres of your cloth seats or carpet piles. You do this by removing it as best you can, and as often as monthly. Particularly if you drive in dusty conditions!

Treat your vinyl and leather.

Use a protectant, as described elsewhere in this book, both on inside and outside plastic, vinyl and rubber surfaces.

'Feed' your leather with the appropriate oils, as included in several leather treatment products. Make sure there's some neat's-foot oil or similar in the product content. You don't want a simpler, wax-based application that just water-proofs. Ask at a good auto supply store or at leather merchant's that is involved in clothing and shoes.

Allow about two hours for these inspections and maintenance.

EVERY SIX MONTHS

Pressure-test the radiator cap and cooling system.

Your garage man can do this. Ensure you get a written record of the pressure reading for your records.

Reverse flush the cooling system.

Of course, this means also adding fresh coolant or filtered water with anti-freeze/anti-boil.

Grease the wheel bearings.

These are often needle-bearings. Remove as much of the old grease as you can with your fingers and replace it with the new stuff, pushing it into all the crevices. Use a high temperature wheel bearing grease.

Check the brake pads for wear.

Your workshop manual will tell you how much or how little thickness of brake pad material is allowable before replacement is needed.

Bleed the brakes.

Brake fluid is hygroscopic – it loves to absorb water from moisture in the air. It goes past wheel cylinder seals and through the very rubber of the hoses. As it absorbs more water, the boiling point of the fluid is reduced, to the extent that it can boil away from contact with the hot brake assembly. This cavitation can occur despite the high pressure applied in the braking system.

Fresh brake fluid renews the full potential of your braking system.

Silicon brake fluid does not absorb water and is longer lasting than the regular stuff. It's more expensive, but will demand less attention over time. Completely bleed out all your brake fluid before replacing it with a silicon type.

Change the automatic transmission fluid.

It can pick up impurities as it works, including tiny metal shavings.

Do a compression test.

A handy device lets you do this yourself. You'll need to turn the engine over multiple times, once for each cylinder. Keep a battery charger handy if your battery has seen better days! Record your results in your logbook.

Check and adjust engine timing.

A timing light and diagnostic device with tachometer helps you do this yourself without having someone read the tachometer gauge on the dash. When ignition points wore away, this operation was quite necessary, but with electronic ignitions, much less so.

Clean and load-test the battery.

You can keep the terminals clean with a spray of WD40 or similar and a thin coating of grease. If there are plastic covers for the leads, keep them on. Load-testing is best and quickest if done by an auto electrician.

Test spark plug wires for resistance.

With a multi-function instrument that tests electrical resistance, this is possible, otherwise testing should be done by an auto electrician. It may solve the mystery of the high-speed missing you may have noticed.

Inspect suspension bushings.

Are they torn or perished? These take a lot of punishment, particularly the front ones. Apart from cornering forces and impacts, grease and oil can attack the integrity of these bushes. Synthetic rubber and even neoprene have their limits, and bushings prevent metal-to-metal contact that can lead to even further suspension damage. Be sure to replace damaged ones as soon as you can.

Do the shock absorber bounce test.

Place your weight onto a corner of your car or truck with your hands and push. Does it rebound and stop? Does it bounce more than once? If the latter, your shock absorbers are not controlling the movement of the vehicle and need replacement. Koni and some other absorber manufacturers make adjustable shocks. These can be tailored to suit your ride preferences or vehicle mass.

If you happen to be at the wrecker's and you find a low-mileage car there of the same make and model as yours, you may be able to remove its shock absorbers and use them yourself. This also applies for hood and hatchback hydraulic struts.

Make sure that you are actually removing shocks from a low-mileage car – it should be accident-damaged (otherwise why is it there?) and the pedals should not look worn. If the pedals are worn, then the odometer has likely gone around the clock once already.

McPherson struts are integral with the springs and the coils could be under load, depending on how the wrecked vehicle lies. Unbolting them yourself should be avoided unless you have professional help in extricating them.

Rotate tyres (if applicable).

You don't need to do this as often unless you put in extraordinary mileage over the previous six months. Just make sure that all tyres receive an even amount of wear. Front-wheel drive cars are particularly hard on the front tyres and easy on the rear, because the front wheels do most of the braking forces (weight transfer to the front) steering and driving. Make sure that if you have uni-directional tyre treads that they are rotating the right way.

Don't forget the spare tyre – bring it out and give one of its brothers a sleeping holiday in its place. You want all five tyres to have the same amount of wear and to be ready to be replaced together. That way you don't need to find and buy the same brand and model of tyres twice over an unknown period of time. If not, you can buy a pair of tyres at a time. If replacing a pair, place either on the front or on the back, never two on one side.

Keep the tyre types identical or as close as possible in terms of tread design and pattern. You want them all to work together in a similar fashion.

Check brake, clutch and accelerator pedals for free play.

Reduce that looseness in the last movement of pedal travel before it 'bites'. This could be done at a 'pedal box' structure under the dashboard or you may have to crawl underneath.

Check exhaust system for leaks, broken hangers and rust.

Mild steel, acids and moisture will attack any exhaust system and if it's not stainless steel, it will need replacing sooner or later. Having said that, some parts of the exhaust system never collect water when cold and never seem to rust away. Listen for that characteristic hissing sound that may indicate a leak in your exhaust system. It may mean simply that a joint is coming apart and some tightening will fix it. Muffler putty is useful here for ensuring a joint is air-tight, but don't go overboard with it.

Check for broken hangers, which may be metal or rubber. The rubber ones may go brittle and part. A droopy or loosely swinging exhaust pipe invariably indicates that it is not held properly. Avoid the embarrassment and inconvenience of dropping your exhaust system on the freeway! Attend to your hangers.

Check the body undercoat.

Old undercoat can go brittle and flake away, revealing the primer on the metal underneath, or even – shock, horror – naked metal itself. Undercoat in a wheel arch can even be worn away in a patch if the wheel/tyre combination fitted is too big for the wheel housing. This will show itself when reversing or on full lock, or if the suspension springs have sagged. It would probably be a combination of several of these causes. Use this discovery to carry your investigations further!

When finding missing undercoat, prepare the surface and coat it as soon as possible. (Choose from among the methods described elsewhere in this edition.). Don't forget it or you may have to deal with a greater rust hole problem further down the track.

Degrease or steam clean the engine compartment.

(You can apply the methods described in this book using a selection of cheap degreasers). It helps to keep your engine bay clean and your local garage mechanic will respect you more and perhaps take better care, because you do. Also, you're not giving him the Oily Mess From Hell as a working environment. He'll be able to pinpoint for you where the oil is coming from, for later attention.

You can also spot potential problems more easily yourself in a relatively clean engine bay.

Wash and wax the body.

Of course. This is a no-brainer, but you'd be surprised at how little care people give to an expensive asset like a car or truck. Regular washing and waxing helps to protect the car and you will spot tiny paint chips sooner, and repair them before the exposed metal underneath starts rusting.

Allow about five hours for these checks and maintenance.

The yearly total is about 60 hours, but this is mostly spread out over a weekly and monthly schedule. It seems like a lot but once you have performed the same thing repeatedly, you will become quicker and more proficient at it.

Remember, the above maintenance schedule is an ideal situation. You may not want to spend so much time doing these tasks. There may be times when life simply gets in the way, and you find that you have missed some or all of these scheduled checks, adjustments and repairs.

Don't kick yourself over it. Just pick up with the next scheduled maintenance.

An occasional lapse will mean that you are still ahead of nearly everyone else in their car and truck maintenance, and that your four-wheeled pride and joy will outlast theirs, giving the maximum of service that it was designed to.

APPENDIX C: A WORD ON ALCOHOL IN FUEL

Ethanol: Fuel or Fool?

Unless you live under a rock (in which case you would be unlikely to run a car) you have heard about the increasing use of ethanol to extend fuel. There are reasons for and against using food crops to create ethanol fuel. There are reasons for and against the use of ethanol as a fuel. We'll focus on the latter issue.

Ethanol is a renewable resource, but delivers less chemical energy per weight than petroleum or gasoline. If the price of the ethanol blend isn't much lower than straight petrol, you will end up paying more for less chemical energy.

It can scrub out flakes of rust and debris from the bottom of the fuel tank, so that they will enter the fuel intake line and potentially clog it. An inline fuel filter will normally take care of this problem but will need to be changed more often.

Ethanol in fuel will also attack certain plastics or rubbers that were designed for immersion in petrol but not in alcohol.

If you have an E85 fuel, that is, an 85% alcohol / 15% petrol blend, available in your area, avoid it. The only exception is if you know for certain that your vehicle is designed to take a high alcohol content in its fuel. Fuel sensors might mistake an E85 blend as a 'system too lean' situation and an alert lamp will glow accusingly on your dashboard.

An E10 ethanol blend (10% ethanol) should be fine in the majority of fuel systems but check internet forums that specify your make and model if you want to be absolutely sure. You can try a tankful of ethanol blend followed by a tankful of straight petrol and see if you can pick a difference in running or acceleration. You may need to replace all your fuel hoses sooner rather than later. Check your fuel injectors or carburettor for alcohol compatibility. Some carburettors had plastic floats, which would probably dissolve in an ethanol-laced fuel. Fuel tank sender unit floats are vulnerable as well. Some metal alloys as sometimes found in carburettors suffer too.

If you trust the bureaucrats, the Environmental Protection Agency of the United States of America have authorized the sale of E15 to vehicles made in 2001 and later. Take greater care if you drive a pre-2001 vehicle. I suspect that an E15 blend may bring you more grief than it's worth.

Boaties are concerned with E15 blends because of the ethanol's ability to bind with water, collecting it together in the bottom of a boat's fuel tank. With an ethanol blend, water may accumulate in your fuel tank, separating out from the petrol. This may give you problems if any of the following applies to you:

If you have an older, unsealed fuel tank or fuel system;

If you live in a high-humidity environment (such as on a coast);

If you don't use your vehicle for a month or more.

Here's how the chemistry works: an ethanol-blend fuel absorbs moisture until the alcohol reaches its saturation point. This is about a teaspoon of water per litre of petrol. When that happens, the ethanol and moisture separates out from the fuel. This is called (predictably) phase separation.

Drivability will suffer, starting may become difficult and there may even be eventual engine damage.

If you have a pool of water/alcohol in the bottom of your fuel tank, there is no option but to drain the tank and dispose of the fuel.

If you're storing your vehicle for lengthy periods of time, this is the best way. Fill your tank up to prevent a large surface area interface with air. This will prevent condensation of water out of the atmosphere from gathering in your tank over time. This works with a vented tank system too.

Add a fuel stabilizer to your tank. Ethanol absorbs moisture but another alcohol such as propanol emulsifies it. That is, it breaks it up and helps it to evaporate. The moisture is then spread throughout the fuel and is prevented from collecting. Stabilisers contain isopropyl alcohol or 2-propanol as it's also called. This is the prime ingredient and purpose of a fuel stabilizer.

Incidentally, isopropyl alcohol is also the basis of fuel line anti-freezes, which are designed to absorb water, preventing it from freezing in cold climates.

Lead Replacement or Doing Without

Which fuel for your car? Leaded petrol is required in classic cars if they were built before the unleaded petrol era. There are exceptions of course. 1930s cars such as Chryslers, Hudsons or other cars whose engines were cast in high-quality, hard iron, where valve seat recession is minimal or non-existent.

Tetra-Ethyl-Lead was added into automobile fuels from the late 1920s to boost octane ratings (eliminating pre-ignition) so allowing for higher compression engines. You obtain more power from the equivalent fuel if it's a higher compression ratio engine. An automobile is more efficient as a result.

Lead was left as a deposit on valve seats and since it is a rather soft metal, this acted rather like a dry lubricant. Valve spring tension was increased by engineers to reduce the lead buildup and reduce the need for valve grinding maintenance jobs. With improvements in metallurgy, valve grinds became less and less necessary.

When unleaded petrol was introduced, it was to allow catalytic converters to operate and 'clean up' the exhaust. Cat converters have brought their own significant environmental and health problems which are unfortunately beyond the scope of this book.

The potential problem with unleaded fuel for classic cars is valve seat recession, which is the result of the valve head grinding away at the valve seat. Sooner or later this tunneling will prevent the valves from fully closing.

If your classic car will be used with lots of heavy acceleration or for towing a heavy caravan, then you will need to use a lead substitute product. The consensus is that if the car will be used lightly, then a lead substitute will not be required.

Smaller engines such as on a European car will rev faster and work harder generally than larger engined cars, like typical American types of the 1960s and earlier. If you run a smaller car from the pre-unleaded era, you will likely need a lead substitute to add to your fuel, as valve seat recession does happen.

Engine work consisting of replacing the valves and valve seat inserts with substitutes made from a harder alloy called stellite will prevent valve seat recession, allowing the use of unleaded fuels of the appropriate octane level.

High-compression engines from the 1950s and 1960s will tend to knock or ping with hard use, and this pre-ignition should be avoided. A pinging or knocking sound means that it's before the right moment to detonate your fuel/air mixture. This can introduce stresses that can detonate your engine.

For these engines, use a higher octane unleaded fuel (like 98 octane) with a lead substitute. Generally, classic cars with engine compression ratios of 8.5:1 to 9.5:1 and possibly higher will be able to use the available octanes of petrol without problems.

APPENDIX D: TIPS FOR HIGHER FUEL ECONOMY

The world economy is in upheaval. Some countries have fared better than others since the Global Financial Crisis hit in 2008, but fundamental problems have not been addressed and the new normal seems to be a period of increasingly unstable markets, money-printing governments and ongoing recession.

So much for the heads-up on the economy. The reason you have bought this e-book is so that you can restore your ride and keep it maintained by spending less money. As the outlook for Main Street is not too good in the near future, saving some money now is a prudent thing to do.

There are lots of things you can do to save money on fuel. You can drive smoothly and be more featherweight on the 'go' pedal but you probably know all that already. At least you don't have to drive like a snail to save money: often a large engine combined with a tall differential ratio can combine to produce outstanding fuel economy under steady running. The extra power is there for short bursts of passing, climbing steep gradients or other exuberance, but when you are travelling along with the crowd on a busy road, the engine's torque can push you along without you having to use your accelerator.

Here's some other tips for fuel economy during a bad economy.

Only Idle Minds Idle

I can't believe it when I see people sitting in a car, parked somewhere with the engine idling. Their engines are running and their brains are switched off. It should be the other way around.

These people usually have their air-conditioner going, which probably explains why. They may be cool in their shirt sleeves, but each second the engine's running and the vehicle's not actually moving somewhere is a waste of fuel. Maybe it's a company car and they don't pay for the fuel they use. (Memo to managers!) Either way, unless you are stuck in traffic with a real expectation of moving off within the next 30-60 seconds, turn it off. Starting a warm engine takes about the same amount of fuel as idling for 60 seconds.

If you're waiting for your lady to come back with the shopping, shut it off and wind down your windows. She'll be longer than you think and you might just have a cool breeze wafting through your open interior. And it's free.

Get out of the car and stretch your legs. Walk around. Use the down time to plan the rest of the day or do some deep thinking about your life and goals. Too often, we're too preoccupied with the minor stuff to give much attention to the major stuff.

Intelligent Braking

Brakes convert your vehicle's motion into heat, which is then dissipated. It's lost kinetic energy that you spent lots of good fuel to build up.

Use your brakes only when you have to. I'm not saying to roll through a stop sign or plough into something rather than touch the 'stop' pedal, but you can use your vehicle's momentum to carry you up the next hill or coast to a stop at a traffic snag ahead.

Stopping and starting is unavoidable in today's typical driving environments but you can anticipate the next set of stoplights and drive through without stopping, if you simply coast towards them and allow them to turn green.

Drive with about three seconds of space between you and the next vehicle. This will give you more options if something abrupt happens and you will be less likely to have to use your brakes for no apparent reason just because the guy in front does. Increase it to five or six seconds space at freeway speeds.

Wiggling's No Drag

Disc brakes are a wonderful improvement on drums, but unlike drums, don't have return springs for the pads. After every hard braking, wiggle the car once from side to side. This will push the disc pads out very slightly so that they don't touch the discs and drag. This drag could cost you about 2 mpg if you have disc brakes on all four wheels.

Wiggle the car only when safe to do so. No spectacular movements – just enough for an alert passenger to notice.

Open Windows or Air Conditioning?

The air conditioner's compressor is a fluid pump which robs several horsepower off the engine to run, and so increases fuel consumption. Some people drive with windows wound down in hot weather instead of using their air-con in the mistaken belief that it saves fuel. Running with windows wound down increases air drag and turbulence.

Each choice robs you of about 10% fuel mileage. If you have a working air-conditioner, you may as well use it, but you can operate it in bursts of several minutes at a time rather than all the time, if the weather is reasonably mild.

Turn off the air-con when the engine is under heavy load, such as passing or climbing a steep hill. The vehicle interior will stay cool for the short times during which the chill button is off.

Tune-Up with Water

As a result of imperfect combustion, leaky piston oil rings or valve stem seals or simply running too rich, you could have a build-up of carbon in your engine cylinders. These deposits can become red hot during normal operation and pre-ignite your fuel/air mixture before the spark plug does, not to mention the additional wear caused by these deposits on moving metal surfaces.

You can prevent excessive carbon build-up in your engine by tuning it properly and repairing any excessive oil leaks. If you have a slight oil leak that will build up carbon deposits over time, you can buy and use a number of additives that are commonly poured into the fuel.

Or you can use this tune-up tip: take a small, empty soda bottle and fill it with luke-warm water. I prefer a plastic bottle to a glass one, in case you accidentally drop it.

Warm up your engine. If you have a carburettor, remove the air-cleaner lid to gain access to the carby throat. For fuel injection systems, gain access to the throttle body.

Hook up an engine tuning device with a tachometer readout, if you have one. Rev the engine to 1500 rpm and keep the throttle there. (A friend can help here.)

Now slowly pour the water down the carburettor throat or throttle body. Drip it in at no more than a trickle. Watch the rev counter or listen to the engine running. If the engine revs start to drop, pour less water.

(This method will NOT work if your fuel injection plenum does not route the water to all the cylinders.)

Doing this water tune-up every 5,000 miles (8,000 kms) is about optimal to clean out and to prevent excessive carbon deposits from forming in your engine.

Moth Balls and Motors

By modestly advancing your ignition timing, you can increase power and fuel economy but this may raise your engine's fuel octane requirements.

If you have a high-compression, high-performance muscle car, then a high enough octane fuel may simply no longer be available. Or you may want to save money by not buying a higher octane fuel.

One way of alleviating the octane problem and ensuring a smoother combustion is to add pure naphthalene to your fuel. It's easiest to source naphthalene in moth balls!

The very things that are used in wardrobes and closets to prevent moths from dining on your clothes can also give you a slight edge in fuel economy when used with an ignition timing advance.

You MUST ensure that you are purchasing pure naphthalene – not some mixture with extenders. That would simply introduce impurities into your petrol. Read the label!

Carry the moth balls around in your vehicle in their sealed package. When filling up, add just ONE naphthalene ball for every 5 U.S. gallons (20 litres or 4.4 Imperial gallons) of fuel. DO NOT ADD MORE.

The downside with too much naphthalene is that it attacks the protective oil film in your cylinders. This is the only thing that prevents metal-to-metal contact between your piston rings and cylinder walls, which would grind them both away quite quickly.

The moth balls will take longer to dissolve in colder weather, so if you are covering many miles and re-filling often, consider not putting them in with every fill-up. Avoid a build-up of moth balls in your tank!

If you feel uneasy about this tip, you can compensate by adding a metal conditioner product to your engine oil. This 'plates' your internal wearing surfaces by coating them to a depth of several microns. The surfaces' irregularities are filled in, making for a smoother, harder finish, reducing friction and wear.

Two Coils Burn Oils

Sometimes, you just have to play the cards you've been dealt. In this case, let us say that you're driving a real oil burner, and for reasons of opportunity or cost, you're stuck with it.

You've already installed a set of 'hot' spark plugs to burn up the excess oil and you still have to clean them every 100-150 miles (160-240 kms) to stay running.

You can fix this problem by installing another coil in parallel with the original one. The voltage is the same but the amperage delivered is now double. Work with your auto electrician, who may be able to recommend a coil and do the connections if you're not confident.

(Increasing the voltage from a coil is wasted effort, as the voltage will only rise to the point where a spark will jump the gap in a spark plug. Same gap, same voltage requirement.)

With two coils and double the amperage, excess oil is burnt off the spark plugs and they only require a regular cleaning schedule. The plugs also give a better ignition of the fuel mixture.

The price paid for this setup is that the plugs will 'wear' away quicker, and so need more frequent re-gapping than normal. In the range of spark plug gaps recommended by your service manual, the closer gap uses less voltage and is a longer duration spark. This longer lasting arc is better for fuel mixture ignition. Unfortunately as it wears away, it must be cleaned and re-gapped more often.

If you have a set of old-fashioned points in your distributor, it would be a good idea to install a second condenser there. Place it next to the original. The second condenser will absorb the extra amperage current and prevent the points from arcing.

Now you're burning up that excess oil and running better in the bargain.

Custom Ignition Timing for Factory Correct Performance

Engines have many moving parts, and wherever there is movement, there is wear and tear. Gaps between moving parts increase over time and distance. Increased gaps produce more slack among meshing parts.

Less precision here means that for a high-mileage engine, you will have to modify your tuning parameters away from original factory specifications. This is in order to have the engine perform to original factory specifications. Strange but true.

Set up your timing light and engine diagnostic device with an r.p.m. readout (the latter is not essential if you have a good ear...or two of them).

Firstly, adjust or ensure that your engine's ignition timing is at original factory specs.

Then advance the timing by rotating the distributor while watching your r.p.m. meter. Advance the timing as long as the idle speed is rising. Once the rising stops, retard the ignition back a trifle. The idea is to prevent over-advancing the timing and causing pinging or pre-ignition.

Ignition timing must be advanced a degree for about every 20,000 miles (or 32,000 kms) on the clock. Do this up to a maximum of 5 degrees or 100,000 miles (162,000 kms).

If the idle speed has risen by more than about 250 r.p.m., reduce it accordingly with the adjustment screw.

Breathe Like an Athlete

Professional athletes are better breathers than you and I. They know how to charge themselves up with oxygen before a sprint or how to maintain their body's optimum respiration for longer duration events, such as running or cycling.

Your vehicle's engine is similar. It can huff and puff along with shallow breaths like Donut Joe running after his dog. Or it can perform with the lung-filling power of an Olympian athlete. Which would you prefer?

Traditional air cleaners that sit on top of a carburettor also have a traditional snorkel through which they breathe. Sometimes they have two. That's how you can tell whether it's a performance engine. (Or has pretensions to same.)

By the 1970s, hot air passages were added that took air from around the exhaust manifolds into the air cleaner. These pre-warmed air intakes were a method for bringing engines to efficient operating temperatures faster and also for reducing exhaust emissions. They usually had temperature-sensitive vacuum controls to operate control flaps in the intake snorkels. There was usually an either/or choice of warm air intake or cold air intake.

In any case, a restricted breathing snorkel is a cheap way of silencing the hiss of a carburettor swallowing air. A quieter car pleases most drivers, but this silencing sacrifices horsepower and fuel efficiency. You try breathing through a plastic straw while running a hundred metres sprint. Are you at your best?

The most power output per fuel consumed is obtained with a 'free breathing' engine. When engines are rated for power and torque output by the factory, they do so on a test stand without any air cleaner, exhaust muffler or restriction to breathing at all. In the real world, equipped with a silencing but restricting air cleaner, all that advertised power is not generated by the engine.

You can claim back some of that wasted power. Ignoring an engine's internals and exhaust for a moment, this is best achieved with an unrestricted air flow into the engine. You can reach your own custom compromise between free breathing and silence.

Is your carburettor restricted? You can find out by measuring the area of the carburettor throat and the area of the snorkel (air intake) opening. By rule of thumb, if the snorkel intake area is smaller than your carburettor opening area, the engine is 'throttled' in its breathing and will never give the power output promised by the Madison Avenue salesmen.

Obtaining the area of a square or rectangular shape is easy but a circular shape is trickier. The area of a circle is calculated using the value *pi*, often noted by its Greek letter –

$$\pi$$

Pi represents the ratio of the circumference of any circle to its diameter. This number is expressed as either 22/7 or 3.14159… The number is infinitely regressive because you can calculate it to an infinite number of decimal places and never reach the end. It goes on and on forever.

(The same can be said of some media commentators. They go on and on forever and are also infinitely regressive, but not in a mathematical way.)

Use the formula:

$$\pi r^2$$

where 'r' is the radius of the circle.

If the engine breathing is restricted, here's how to overcome this.

The method is to examine your air cleaner base and the filter element inside. This is like a drum (air cleaner body) with a smaller ring inside (air filter element), with the carburettor inside the air filter 'ring'. Or you might have a rectangular, box-shaped air cleaner with a rectangular filter element inside. The filter element covers the air inlet into the engine.

Determine the gap between the *outside* of the filter element and the *inside* of the air cleaner housing. There's always a space. This is the area in which you will be drilling out a hole or two. The extra air inlets in the air cleaner assembly must be *outside* the filter or you will be sucking in dirty air.

Take your carburettor throat area and subtract your snorkel intake area from it. This gives you the shortfall of intake area you need to open up to ensure free breathing of the carburettor.

Divide this shortfall of area by two. This will give you the areas of two round holes to drill out. You can work backwards to obtain their sizes using pi and the radius. (In some cases, more holes may need to be drilled due to space constraints.)

Using a marker or crayon, mark the sites in the base of the air cleaner housing where you want to drill out the holes. Note that it is the base of the air cleaner, not the sides, where you are drilling the extra holes. This is so that they will be invisible during a casual inspection. This looks neater and is most important if you want to maintain a 'stock' appearance. It's also easier to drill out a usually flat base surface than the curved sides.

Keep the holes away from internal structural supports and vacuum line entry points. Plan the holes so that they are further apart than closer together. You wish to avoid any structural problems caused by taking out so much metal on one side that you weaken the whole housing.

Borrow a hole cutting tool that you can mount on your power drill. If you can, choose a circle size that is matched by an over-the-counter rubber grommet. Buy a couple of said grommets. Never fear, I shall explain why.

Now set up your air cleaner base in a firm position on a stand or vise (remembering to protect the painted surface with rags or masking tape) and drill out the holes with the hole cutting tool.

File away any burrs or sharp edges at the metal cut. Paint on some enamel or lacquer to cover the exposed metal and prevent it from rusting later. Drilling holes from the base of the air cleaner housing also has an added benefit: the paint you apply is purely utilitarian. As the holes are not visible, you need not cover the edges with a colour-matched paint. If the air cleaner housing is black anyway, it's easy to colour-match that!

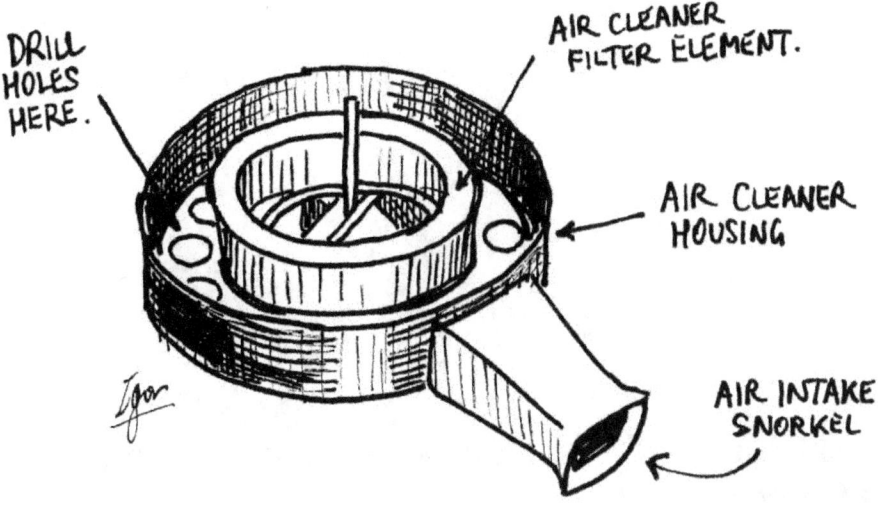

Assemble the air cleaner and its element and attach any additional hoses, etc. Are the new breathing holes visible? Does it all sit as well as before? Start the engine and let it idle. If warm, rev it up a little and listen. Do you detect any extra noise, such as a hiss? If so, do you barely hear it or is it loud and clear?

If your vehicle has a noise insulator pad under the bonnet (or 'hood') close the hood and listen. Sit down in the driver's seat, shut all the doors and windows and listen. Do you still hear any extra noise?

This is the acid test. Take a short drive and use your heater / ventilator fan or air conditioner, but not your radio. This gives you an idea of the background ensemble of sounds that is your vehicle, that subtle symphony of noises that you know the best. Can you hear a difference now?

Are you happy with the result? Do you hear any increased noise at all? If you do, is it subtle enough that you are happy to live with it?

If, in the final analysis, you feel that any extra noise is clear enough to be irritating, you can use one of those rubber grommets you bought (remember?) and close up one of the breather holes. This may reduce the extra noise to a whisper or below your hearing level.

Now (if not before), you can smile with satisfaction at your increased power or fuel economy (or both) and just as much comfort as ever.

APPENDIX E: FURTHER RESOURCES FOR HIGH FUEL ECONOMY

For the more mechanically advanced, there are more methods available that can radically increase fuel economy for almost any vehicle. Some of the simpler tips which did not involve fabrication or modifications are included here.

Further manuals and kits are available for building and using water injectors, Brown's Gas generators, carburettor enhancers or other devices to boost your fuel economy. Some of these devices only require inexpensive, off-the-shelf parts. Further information can be found by going to the Eagle-Research website here:

https://www.eagle-research.com/cms/af/ispajic

Copy and paste this address into your browser. To be absolutely straight with you, if you purchase a book or manual, my cartoonist will receive a small commission.

ABOUT THE AUTHOR

Steven C. Brooks is not a professional mechanic or panel beater but he is passionate about car restoration. He asserts that it doesn't have to be a full-scale mega-production, but can be done in a series of modest steps. Steve began (as do we all) as a total novice. Starting with maintenance, he moved on to repairs and further into restoration. Steve learned from his own experience restoring cars on shoestring budgets and by helping backyard masters of the mechanical and body arts. Firmly believing in learning from the mistakes of others rather than having to repeat them, Steve Brooks offers the fruits of his and others' mistakes in this series of books.

CONTACT US

If you found this e-book useful with many handy hints or just a load of old tripe, you can contact the author at:

flashpointgrafx@optusnet.com.au

He's happy to receive honest reviews so his next scribblings can improve. You can also reach the illustrator here too – for the same reason!

Visit Steve Brooks' page in Amazon's Author Central at:

https://www.amazon.com/author/stevecbrooks

DISCLAIMER

This e-book is sold for research and / or experimental purposes only. Results will vary according to the reader's knowledge, expertise and experience. All care has been taken by the author to present accurate information. The author, associates of the author and the publisher assume no responsibility for damage or injury resulting from the reader's use or misuse of information, insights, methods or instructions provided herein.

www.ingramcontent.com/pod-product-compliance
Lightning Source LLC
Chambersburg PA
CBHW050313010526
44107CB00055B/2228